D1560129

The Apaches

BIBLIOGRAPHICAL SERIES
The Newberry Library Center
for the History of the American Indian

General Editor
Francis Jennings

The Center Is Supported by Grants from

The National Endowment for the Humanities
The Ford Foundation
The W. Clement and Jessie V. Stone Foundation
The Woods Charitable Fund, Inc.

The Apaches

A Critical Bibliography

MICHAEL EDWARD MELODY

Published for the Newberry Library

Indiana University Press

BLOOMINGTON AND LONDON

Published in Canada by Fitzhenry & Whiteside Limited, Don Mills Ontario

Manufactured in the United States of America

Library of Congress Cataloging in Publication Data
Melody, Michael Edward.
The Apaches: a critical bibliography.
(Bibliographical series)
1. Apache Indians—Bibliography. I. Title. II. Series.
Z1210.A6M44   [E99.A6]   016.970'004'97   77-6918
ISBN 0-253-30764-3   1 2 3 4 5 81 80 79 78 77

CONTENTS

THE EDITOR TO THE READER

A massive literature exists for the history and culture of American Indians, but the quality of that literature is very uneven. At its best it compares well with the finest scholarship and most interesting reading to be found anywhere. At its worst it may take the form of malicious fabrication. Sometimes, well-intentioned writers give false impressions of reality either because of their own limitations of mind or because they lack adequate information. The consequence is a kind of chaos through which advanced scholars as well as new students must warily pick their way. It is, after all, a history of hundreds, if not thousands, of human communities spread over an entire continent and enduring through millennia of pre-Columbian years as well as the five centuries that Europeans have documented since 1492. That is not a small amount of history.

Often, however, historians have been so concerned with the affairs of European colonies or the United States that they have almost omitted Indians from their own history. There is a way of writing "frontier history" and the "history of Indian-White relations" that often focuses so narrowly upon the intentions and desires of Euro-Americans as to treat Native Americans as though they were merely natural parts of the landscape, like forests or mountains or wild animals — obstacles to "progress" or "civilization." One of the major purposes of the Newberry Library's Center for the History of the American Indian is to modify that narrow conception; to put Indians properly back into the central role in their own history and into the history of the United States of America as well — as participants in, rather than obstacles to, the creation of American society and culture.

The series of bibliographies of which this book is one part is intended as a guide to reliable sources and studies in particular fields of the general literature. Some of these are devoted to culture areas; others treat selected individual tribes; and a third group speaks to significant contemporary and historical issues.

These are the classifications made by scholars trying to sort order out of the multitude of ways in which Indians have lived. The Apaches, however, have a historical identity that fits badly into categories. They were not indigenous to the territory in which we find them historically; they had immigrated to it probably only a short time before the Spanish conquistadores arrived. They were not organized into coherent tribal political entities; their lives were ordered in small kin groups for which even the term "band" seems inflated. They moved around a lot. Our early accounts of them are fragmentary, often fantastic, and sometimes utterly fabricated. But they knew their own people and their own ways, and Dr. Melody has now provided a guide by means of which students may penetrate the mysteries in the available literature and avoid the trash.

This work is designed in a format, standard for the series, intended to be useful to both beginning students and advanced scholars. It has two main parts: the essay (conveniently organized by subheadings) and an alphabetical list of all works cited. All citations in the essay are directly keyed, by means of bracketed numbers, to the more complete publication data in the list; and each item in the list carries a cross-reference to the page number where it is mentioned in the essay. In addition, the series incorporates several information-at-a-glance features. Among them are two sets of recommended titles: a list of five works recommended for the beginner and a group of volumes that constitute a basic library collection in the field. The large, complete list also uses asterisks to denote works suitable for secondary school students. This apparatus has been built in because the bibliographical essay, in a form familiar to scholars, could prove fairly hard going for beginners, who may wish to put it aside until they have gained sufficient background from introductory materials. Such students should come back to the essay eventually, however, because it surveys a vast sweep of information about a great variety of persons, places, communities, and events.

There is variety also in the kinds of sources because these critical bibliographies support the study of ethnohistory. Unlike older, more narrow disciplines, ethnohistory embraces the entire culture of a people; it demands contributions from a wide range of source materials. Not the least of these in the history of American Indians are their own music, crafts, linguistics, and oral traditions. Whenever possible, the authors have included such sources as well as those associated with politics, economics, geography, and so on. It will be recognized that the variety of relevant sources will change with the nature of the topic discussed.

In the last analysis this work, like all other bibliographical devices, is a tool. Each author is an expert who knows the literature and advises what source is most helpful for which purpose, but students must use this help according to their individual purposes and capacities. Many ways suggest themselves. The decision is the reader's own.

INTRODUCTION

"Apache! Apache!" Often the cry came too late. Frequently, as old accounts note, the moment of recognition was also the moment of death. Cunning and martial prowess enabled the Apaches to terrorize the Southwest, and at times murder and thievery caused such general insecurity about life and property that settlers vacated an entire area. As John C. Cremony wrote: "Settlers have been driven out time and again; mines of almost fabulous richness have been abandoned; from Tucson to El Paso, three hundred miles, is one continuous graveyard, marked throughout the whole distance with the grim and silent monuments of death from Apache animosity" [49, p. 204]. Overall, in the popular view the Apaches are known as bloodthirsty savages. Apache Pass has been blazoned on the American consciousness as a locus of carnage and destruction — a place of horror marked by sadistic tortures and cruel deaths, whose red soil might be no accident. In the pass, quarter was neither given nor expected.

But this popular view, though perpetuated and even enhanced by children's games such as Fort Apache and by television serials like Rin Tin Tin, is decidedly one-sided, if not actually false. The Apaches, often themselves the victims of deception, dishonest Indian agents, governmental inertia, treachery, murder, and massacre, fought nobly for their land, families, and way of life. Born and nurtured in a harsh environment, they used stealth and cunning as their natural weapons. Though never great in number, they were more than a match for the United States army, and not until the army employed Apaches as scouts (for only an Apache could track another Apache), were the People finally subjugated. Geronimo, one of the most celebrated Apache warriors, surrendered for the last time in 1886.

The Apaches

The Apaches arrived in the Southwest between A.D. 1000 and 1500 — no one is certain how long before the Spaniards came. Jack D. Forbes, in his *Apache, Navaho, and Spaniard* [72], persuasively argues for an earlier date than is accepted by most other scholars, Hodge and Schroeder, for example, but the accepted interpretation places the arrival of the Apaches relatively close to that of the Spaniards. The Apaches formed a small part of a larger migration of linguistically related peoples that in turn was a fragment of a vast continental migration. They journeyed from north to south, though the route itself cannot be precisely determined. Regardless of these uncertainties, experts are certain that the Apaches were well established in the area by the time of Coronado's arrival.

The term Apache is a misnomer. They called themselves the *N'de, Dini, Tinde,* or *Inde,* meaning simply the people, and the term Apache, by which they have been known since 1598, is probably derived from the Zuñi name for the Navaho, *Ápachu,* which means enemy.

Considered linguistically, the Apaches are part of the

southern division of the Athapascan linguistic stock, to which the Navahos also belong. The Athapascan group forms the most widely dispersed linguistic family in North America; parts of this family can be found not only in the Southwest, but also in Alaska, Canada, and along the Northwest coast. The latter area comprises the earliest known homeland of the group.

In the latter half of the fifteenth century the Athapascan groups in the Southwest divided into smaller units that spread over a vast territory. *Gran Apacheria*, as the Spaniards sometimes called it, included all of New Mexico and parts of Texas, Colorado, Kansas, Arizona, Oklahoma, and Northern Mexico, an area approximately seven hundred miles wide and six hundred long.

On linguistic grounds the Southern Athapascans are typically divided into two major groups. The eastern group comprises the Jicarilla, Lipan, and Kiowa (Apaches). The western includes the Chiricahua, Mescalero, and Western Apaches. Linguistically, the Navahos are considered part of the Western Apachean group, though they have always been treated separately. Thus, strictly delimited, the Apachean tribal group includes the Jicarilla, Lipan, Kiowa (Apaches), Chiricahua, Mescalero, and Western Apaches.

Life was difficult for the Apaches, for nature was not bounteous, and the dry, cracked land yielded its fruit grudgingly. The image of a Thanksgiving feast with smiling Pilgrims and friendly Indians around a table laden with food would seem inappropriate among the cacti. The century plant, with its phallic thrust of fertility and then death, remains the appropriate symbol. The mountains of Arizona and New Mexico, however, did offer some relief. The People lived primarily by hunting, for big game such as deer, elk, antelope, and bison (hunted primarily by the Kiowa Apaches) was plentiful in *Gran Apacheria*. The Apaches also gathered wild plants, including several species of cactus fruit, piñon nuts, mesquite beans, berries, and acorns. The ethnographic record also indicates that the Apaches engaged in a "primitive" type of farming, though not to the extent that they were forced into a sedentary life.

The people generally lived in wickiups, except primarily for the Plains Apaches, who lived in tipis. The *Handbook of American Indians North of Mexico*, edited by Frederick Webb Hodge, describes the wickiup of the Chiricahuas as "a rude brush hut, circular or oval, with the earth scooped out to enlarge its capacity" [94, 1:282]. If the hut was large, a fire could be built in the center to provide warmth in the winter. At least among the Chiricahuas, the wickiups were built close together, and when camp was moved they were burned.

Each Apachean tribal group was composed of bands that in turn were made up of local groups: the basic social, economic, and political unit. Typically, local groups were composed of several related families, though an actual blood relationship was not necessary. At this level of social organization the mother-in-law was a central figure, and obligation tended to be centered in her person. For example, game was brought to one's mother-in-law for cooking as well as for distribution.

The Apaches did not have tribal chiefs. Chiefs led either bands (a historical development) or local groups and were selected by a recognition/emergence process based on the dual claims of heredity and ability. However, the clan system of the Western Apache complicates this skeletal outline, for the Western Apaches did have clan chiefs. Descent was generally traced through the mother, and Apachean culture exhibits matrilocal residence patterns.

The Apaches were warriors. Disputes over trading and hunting rights, retaliation and blood revenge, and territorial encroachments frequently led to warfare. Distinctions within the language suggest that the Apaches differentiated sharply between raiding and warfare. The Apaches often engaged in warfare with the Pawnee, other Plains tribes, and the Pima, Papago, and the Sobaipuri in Arizona as well as the Pueblo tribes in New Mexico. As the Spaniards and their settlements drew closer, the Apaches began to develop a taste for cattle, horses, and mules and made raids to obtain them.

Apachean Bibliography

The Apaches present special bibliographical problems. Unlike many other tribal groups, few if any reliable missionary accounts exist for the Apaches, since they welcomed missionaries into their midst only in recent times. Similarly, reliable and useful accounts by explorers are rare. Small group life in a large territory, frequent camp movements, and a decided hostility toward outsiders all contribute to the dearth of reliable accounts of the aboriginal Apaches. The accounts that do exist often serve only to confuse the situation, since in these accounts non-Apachean groups are sometimes identified as Apaches. The epithet Apache seems to have been applied indiscriminately to any warlike, nomadic group within *Gran Apacheria*. In addition, the old accounts identify Apachean groups by a variety of names [94, 1:63-64]; the nomenclature became somewhat standardized only in recent times. These problems are compounded by the fact that *Gran Apacheria* was formerly under the suzerainty of Spain and Mexico. In addition to language difficulties, the necessity of locating old documents presents serious obstacles to research. The microfilming of various Spanish and Mexican archives has eased this particular problem; yet a further complication arises in that many of the old sources are self-serving fabrications in which fantasy all too often seems the norm. And since war was the usual state of affairs in *Gran Apacheria*, a scarcity of sources regarding the aboriginal way of life of the Apaches is not altogether surprising.

For the period following the United States' acquisition of *Gran Apacheria* the quantity of literature available dramatically increases. War, however, remained the dominant way of life; so the new body of literature largely concerns military matters, and basic ethnographic works remain rare. Accounts originating in the American period, like those of the Spanish and Mexican eras, are also frequently tainted by self-serving considerations.

Since only a few Apaches have told their own stories, the seriousness of this situation is further compounded.

In this same period the Apaches were herded onto reservations. The aboriginal way of life slowly disappeared, somewhat forgotten by the People and never really known or understood by the land-hungry white men. Thus, studies of aboriginal Apachean history and ethnology are usually reconstructions compiled from many sources. For many historical periods and ethnographic areas reconstruction has not been possible, and ignorance prevails.

Anthropological fieldwork among the Apachean groups did not begin until the 1930s. The Geronimo wars lasted until the late 1880s, and the hostile and suspicious Apaches were not easy to study. Stories still circulate in anthropological circles about the mysterious death of one fieldworker among the Apaches, and the persistence of such stories reflects the hesitancy, or outright fear, of researchers [87, n. 17]. Most of the scholarly literature on the Apaches is the work of a relatively few anthropologists. Primary among these are Grenville Goodwin and Morris Opler. As Edward Spicer wrote [20, p. 3]:

To GRENVILLE GOODWIN we owe most of what understanding we have of the way of life of the Western Apaches. Few have tried seriously to learn what that way of life was, and even fewer have written effectively about it. The abundant literature on the Western Apaches, inspired in great part by the spectacular forays of Geronimo and his predecessors, is largely a literature of the white man who fought the Indians and participated in the final, relentless roundups. It is not a literature from which emerges a view of the values by which Apaches lived. But for the work of Goodwin, we would have lost almost all opportunity to participate in the Apache world.

It is appropriate to add: And but for the work of Morris Opler.

RECOMMENDED WORKS

For the Beginner

[23]   Jason Betzinez, with Wilbur S. Nye. *I Fought with Geronimo*.

[107] James Kaywaykla. *In the Days of Victorio*.

[112] Frank C. Lockwood. *The Apache Indians*.

[119] Thomas E. Mails. *The People Called Apache*.

[191] John Upton Terrell. *Apache Chronicle*.

[194] Dan L. Thrapp. *The Conquest of Apacheria*.

For a Basic Library Collection

[6]   Gordon Baldwin. *The Warrior Apaches*.

[17]   Keith H. Basso. *Western Apache Witchcraft*.

[20]   Keith H. Basso, ed. *Western Apache Raiding and Warfare*.

[28]   John G. Bourke. *An Apache Campaign in the Sierra Madre*.

[29]   John G. Bourke. *On the Border with Crook*.

[30]   John G. Bourke. *The Medicine-Men of the Apache*.

[35]   Charles S. Brant, ed. *Jim Whitewolf: The Life of a Kiowa Apache*.

[43]   Woodworth Clum. *Apache Agent: The Story of John P. Clum*.

[50]   John C. Cremony. *Life among the Apaches*.

[55]   John C. Cremony. *General George Crook, His Autobiography*. Edited and annotated by Martin F. Schmitt.

[72]   Jack D. Forbes. *Apache, Navaho, and Spaniard*.

[85]   Grenville Goodwin. *The Social Organization of the Western Apache*.

[89]   Dolores A. Gunnerson. *The Jicarilla Apaches, A Study in Survival*.

[111]   Frank C. Lockwood. *Pioneer Days in Arizona*.

[141]   Morris E. Opler. *An Apache Life-Way*.

[154]   Morris E. Opler. "An Outline of Chiricahua Apache Social Organization."

BIBLIOGRAPHICAL ESSAY

General Reference Works

Frederick W. Hodge, ed., *Handbook of American Indians North of Mexico* [94] continues to be the basic source for all native American ethnographers. Published in two volumes, the text is arranged alphabetically. Entries are included for each of the tribal groupings — Apaches, for example — as well as for particular tribes such as the Jicarillas and Chiricahuas. Individual articles deal with items and concepts such as pipes, religion, and mythology. In addition, the *Handbook* includes lists of alternate names for the various tribes. In regard to the Apaches the *Handbook*, published in 1907–10, contains some outdated information. For example, its assertion that the Kiowa Apaches do not represent a detached band of Athapascan origin has been corrected by Charles Brant in his "The Cultural Position of the Kiowa-Apache" [31]. Similarly, some of the concepts analyzed reflect ethnocentric biases; an illustration of this is the treatment of government. For an extended discussion of this point see Michael E. Melody's "The Sacred Hoop" [123]. With these strictures in mind, the *Handbook* remains the most compact, readily available source. A new edition is now in preparation. John Swanton's *The Indian Tribes of North America* [188], another basic reference work, is arranged geographically and includes basic data such as population and alternate names of various groups.

Harold Driver's *Indians of North America* [63] furnishes a great deal of comparative material. Conceptually organized, this work includes material concerning Apache kinship, life cycle, music, ritual, subsistence, warfare, and so forth.

Dee Brown, in *Bury My Heart at Wounded Knee: An Indian History of the American West* [36], points out the general inadequacies of the standard works of American history. An exception is Jacob P. Dunn's 1886 book *Massacres of the Mountains* [64], reprinted in 1958. This book treats the Native American dealings with the white man in an accurate, sympathetic manner. Dunn includes a chapter on the Oatman massacre and captivity as well as a more general chapter on Apachean history. Besides its contribution to Apachean historiography, *Massacres of the Mountains* furnishes a context for understanding Apachean-American relations. As Dunn concludes, "the policy of extermination in Arizona, coupled with concentration in New Mexico, proved a dismal failure, after a full and fair trial" [64, p. 341]. In standard histories the native American is usually viewed as an adjunct to what is essentially the white man's story. Dee Brown's work, as the subtitle indicates, focuses on the native American per se. This book, however, tends to be excessively apologetic owing to a very selective presentation of the material. Two chapters of *Bury My Heart at Wounded Knee* include Apachean history. The first considers general matters, such as the Camp Grant Massacre and the murder of Mangas Coloradas, and the second treats the reservation period, focusing on the Geronimo wars.

I Have Spoken [5], compiled by Virginia Irving Armstrong, and *Indian Oratory* [217], compiled by W. C. Vanderwerth, both anthologies of Indian speeches, provide important background for any reading of American history. These powerful, eloquent speeches embody the Indian reaction to the white man. Taken together, they also present the Indians' articulation of their own values and way of life in the face of cultural genocide. Both works include speeches and remarks by individual Apaches, such as Cochise, and the notes in *I Have Spoken* are especially helpful.

Basic Ethnographic Works

Primary

S. M. Barrett's *Geronimo's Story of His Life* [13], reprinted in 1970 as *Geronimo, His Own Story*, is generally regarded as a basic authoritative source for Apachean ethnography and history. While Geronimo himself told the story orally, Barrett, with the aid of translators, made an English transcription of the warrior's speeches. This translation, including notes by Barrett, supposedly constitutes Geronimo's autobiography. The book does include a great deal of seemingly valuable information, but Morris Opler has recently cast doubt on its authoritativeness. One of Opler's informants was present while Geronimo's words were being translated. According to this informant (a man known to be reliable), the translated text and Geronimo's spoken words varied a good deal. The translator, it seems, was an ornery person. In addition, Opler maintains that the text does not even adequately reflect Chiricahua custom; many of Geronimo's remarks about Apachean government vary from known Chiricahua practice. Thus the Barrett volume, in spite of its wide popular use, must be approached with serious reservations and cannot be uncritically accepted as Geronimo's authentic autobiography.

I Fought with Geronimo [23], another widely accepted work, written by Jason Betzinez in collaboration with Wilbur S. Nye, is especially interesting because it deals with the transition from the aboriginal Chiricahua way of life through the confinement period to the reservation stage at Fort Sill. Equally worthy of note is the description of Jason's education at Carlisle Indian School. By the end of the book Jason becomes a tragic figure, for though educated as a white man, he nonetheless remains an Apache. Though he longs for acceptance by white men, he really belongs to neither world. This book thus contains an implicit case study of acculturation and cultural dissolution as well as a general ethnography and history.

Eve Ball's editing of *In the Days of Victorio* [107] is grounded upon the recollections of James Kaywaykla, a member of the Warm Springs band of the Chiricahua Apaches. Though primarily a history of the Warm Springs band in the bloody period of the late nineteenth century, the text includes a great deal of ethnologic material, especially in the areas of religion and ritual. The descriptions of Lozen's use of her power to locate the enemy and the many vignettes of the aboriginal Chiricahua way of life are particularly interesting. Ball's work is securely grounded upon both historical and ethnological fact. Related works, also primarily historical in approach, include Kaywaykla's "I Survived the Massacre of Tres Castillos" [105] and his "Nana's People" [106], articles that also focus on the Chiricahua tribal group.

Jim Whitewolf: The Life of a Kiowa Apache [35] contains the major ethnography of this Apachean tribe. The dearth of reliable scholarly works on this group underscores the importance of this particular book. Though done in an autobiographical fashion, it includes a large amount of ethnographic information. Charles Brant's introductory essay on Kiowa Apache culture is especially helpful.

The Mescaleros are represented by Morris Opler's *Apache Odyssey: A Journey between Two Worlds* [157]. Also done in an autobiographical mode, this book presents not only an ethnography, but also a case study of acculturation. Opler's introductory essay contains a major summary of Mescalero Apache culture, and extensive comparative footnotes are included within the text.

Ciyé "Niño" Cochise's *The First Hundred Years of Niño Cochise* [44] has also had wide circulation. Some authorities, however, regard this book as spurious. As in the case of the Barrett volume, evidence for this position arises from the text itself. Besides the incredible nature of Niño's story, the book includes items that are at variance with known Chiricahua practice, for instance, the treatment of clans. Similarly, the role of the shaman as presented by Niño is contradicted by reliable Chiricahua ethnographies. Thus, most anthropological and historical authorities on the Apaches disregard this book. Niño claims that he is not only a Chiricahua, but also the grandson of Cochise. Several authorities, however, will not even grant that he is an Apache. By implication, "Apache Tears," an article by Niño Cochise and A. K. Griffith [45], must also be taken with due caution.

Secondary

A variety of old pieces deal at least tangentially with Apachean ethnography. The work of John C. Cremony, an author typically cited in studies of Apachean history and ethnography, represents the core of this older body of literature. His "Some Savages" [51] includes material on the Bascom affair, and "The Apache Race" [49] presents one of the few sympathetic treatments of the Apaches written in the nineteenth century. Both pieces include ethnological material of some importance, especially in the area of government. *Life among the Apaches* [50], reprinted in 1969, is Cremony's most important contribution. Written in a loose autobiographical fashion, the work narrates many of the most significant events of the latter part of the nineteenth century and also includes a good deal of ethnological material. Cremony, however, is not always a reliable source of facts or interpretation. His work, as accepted as it is, must be used with some caution [e.g., 197, p. 338, n. 7; p. 339, n. 17] Material of a similar nature is found in Frederick Schwatka's "Among the Apaches" [178]. *The Land of Poco Tiempo*, by Charles F. Lummis [115], contains ethnological and historical material worthy of note, especially on the Apachean mode of warfare. The comparison of Apachean and ancient Greek warfare is especially provocative. James O. Pattie, "Pattie's Personal Narrative" [164], includes an account of a meeting with Apaches at the Santa Rita copper mines. The Apaches professed peaceful intentions toward the Americans but showed only enmity for the Spaniards and Mexicans. The copper mines are often at the center of early American relations with the Apaches, especially the Chiricahuas. Edward Palmer's "Notes on Indian Manners and Customs" [162] deals with general concerns such as marriage customs. Several contemporary authors report the older descriptions of the Apaches. These include "Cordero's Description of the Apache", edited by Daniel S. Matson and Albert H. Schroeder [121], and Jack Forbes's "The Early Western Apache, 1300–1700" [73].

A variety of more recent works treat the Apachean group as a whole. Thomas E. Mails's *The People Called Apache* [119] summarizes the current state of the anthropological literature. Though a popularization, this book serves as a comprehensive introduction to the subject. "The Apache," an introductory piece prepared by the Federal Writers' Project in Arizona [69], is designed as an "aid" to both teachers and laymen. Frank C. Lockwood's *The Apache Indians* [112] has long been accepted as an important source of Apachean history and ethnology, but more contemporary scholars have demonstrated that some of Lockwood's material is in error. Edward H. Spicer's *Cycles of Conquest* [186], a much lauded work, synthesizes a great amount of data concerning the greater Southwestern tribes. He presents a far-ranging study of acculturation and diffusion, focusing mainly on one fundamental question: "What are the chief ways in which Indians have responded to Western civilization and what has happened to their cultures as a result of contact?" Spicer, however, deals explicitly only with the Western Apaches. More narrow general works include Miles M. Collier's "Apache Laws" [47] and Elizabeth B. Hagberg's "Southwestern Indian Burial Practices" [91]. Collier's brief piece deals mainly with the means of settling disputes. Hagberg's thesis, completed as the period of fieldwork among the Apaches was just beginning, presents a broad comparative context for understanding Apachean burial practices, and complements Opler's more recent findings. Albert Schroeder's "A Study of the Apache Indian," recently published [213], is an excellent source for Apachean history and ethnology, and Schroeder's familiarity with manuscript items makes it especially interesting. The Indian Claims Commission cases provided the impetus for his study. The scholarly works generated by the Indian Claims Commission contain a vast amount of historical and ethnographic information, but one must remember that these studies form part of an adversary proceeding and usually focus on the extent of Apachean territory and land use. *Apache Kinship Systems*, by Robert N. Bellah [22], a broadly comparative work, deals with the kinship systems of the Jicarilla, Kiowa (Apaches), Chiricahua, Lipan, Mescalero, and Western Apaches. This work is generally regarded as a standard source. In "Apachean Culture: A Study in Unity and Diversity," James H. and Dolores A. Gunnerson [90] bring archeological evidence to bear upon questions of Apachean migration patterns and material culture, focusing on several perennial issues in Apachean historiography. Gordon Baldwin's *The Warrior Apaches* [6], also a general work, deals primarily with the Chiricahua and Western Apaches. "Designed to fill the long existing need for a description, on the adult level, of the aboriginal life of the Apaches," as the foreword says, this book includes a good deal of ethnographic information, especially in the areas of government, social life, and religion. It is marred, however, by a lack of documentation, and Baldwin has a tendency to overstate his case.

Western Apachean Ethnography

As previously noted, Grenville Goodwin is responsible for most of our knowledge of the Western Apaches. His *The Social Organization of the Western Apache* [85] has become the standard work on this group. In addition to a historical overview, this book includes material on kinship, marriage customs, clans, and life stages. *Western Apache Raiding and Warfare*, Goodwin's other major work, was edited from his notes by Keith H. Basso [20]. Besides some work on the religion of the Western Apaches, Goodwin's other major contribution consists of his studies of the clan system of the Western Apaches. These studies include "Clans of the Western Apache" [82] and "The Characteristics and Function of Clan in a

Southern Athapascan Culture" [83]. Both articles, however, are somewhat cursory. *Grenville Goodwin among the
Western Apache: Letters from the Field* [87], a recent book
edited by Morris E. Opler, provides the context for his
work and an implicit history of his research efforts as well
as ethnographic data.

Keith H. Basso must be regarded as another major
ethnographer of the Western Apaches. Besides his work
in Apachean religion and ritual, his relatively recent
book *The Cibecue Apache: Case Studies in Cultural Anthropology* [18] is a contribution to Western Apachean ethnography as well as to anthropological theory. His " 'To
Give Up on Words': Silence in Western Apache Culture"
[19] is a study of the linguistic context of silence. Aleš
Hrdlička's "Notes on the San Carlos Apache" [101] and
Charles Smart's "Notes on the 'Tonto' Apaches" [181],
two brief pieces, represent contributions of decidedly
less importance. These pieces do include material concerning acculturation, though the authors' interests are
primarily general and descriptive.

Albert B. Reagan's "Notes on the Indians of the Fort
Apache Region" [170] secures his status as a student of
Western Apachean culture. Both highly descriptive and
comprehensive, this piece is based upon work at the
American Museum of Natural History (New York), the
Field Columbian Museum (Chicago), and the National
Museum of Natural History, Smithsonian Institution.
His other published works, mostly in obscure journals,
deal mainly with games. Among these are "The Moccasin
Game" [169], "The Apache Stick Game" [167], "The

Apache Medicine Game" [168], and "Naëzhosh; or, the
Apache Pole Game" [166]. These short articles also de-
vote a good deal of attention to detail. Reagan's treatment of the moccasin game, for example, is one of the
few that focus, however briefly, on the role of chance in
the outcome. His interest in the Apaches presumably
germinated during his brief period of work for the Indian Service at Fort Apache, about 1901–02. His accu-
racy has been questioned, however.

Contributions to an understanding of Western Apachean material culture are represented by, among
others, Ralph Beals's *Material Culture of the Pima, Papago,
and Western Apache* [21]. Winfred Buskirk's "Western
Apache Subsistence Economy" [38] contains an elaborate
and complete study of the subsistence patterns of the
Western Apache, and Homer Aschmann's "Environment and Ecology in the 'Northern Tonto' Claim Area"
[201], a study sparked by the Indian Claims Commission,
delimits the subsistence economy of the Northern
Tontos in relation to their environment.

Studies of acculturation include: Inez H. Capps's
"Social Change among the White Mountain Apache Indians" [39], Harry T. Getty's "The San Carlos Indian
Cattle Industry" [77], and Michael W. Everett's "White
Mountain Apache Medical Decision-Making" [67]. Edward A. Parmee's *Formal Education and Culture Change*
[163], an angry piece of writing, studies the educational
system at the San Carlos reservation. According to Parmee, the study demonstrates "how education, when used
to impose cultural change at a rate and of a nature that is

defined solely by the convenience and ethnocentric policies of the dominant culture, can create serious social and psychological conflicts within the minority society." The result is that the victims are left "morally weakened, culturally deprived, and economically dependent" [163, p. 1].

Morris E. Opler, as was previously noted, is mainly responsible for our knowledge of the Apachean way of life. His *An Apache Life-Way* [141] is an excellent piece of ethnography whose power arises from Opler's abundant use of informants' accounts. The organization of the book in terms of the life cycle of an individual does, however, present difficulties when a researcher attempts to grapple with the work conceptually. This basic ethnography is supplemented by Opler's short article "Notes on Chiricahua Apache Culture" [153], which, as he points out, adds detail and nuance to *An Apache Life-Way*, and by his "An Outline of Chiricahua Apache Social Organization" [154], which deals conceptually with much of the ethnographic information presented in *An Apache Life-Way*. Michael E. Melody's "The Sacred Hoop" [123] analyzes the interrelationships between physical environment, mythology, religion, ritual, and government among the Chiricahua Apaches. William G. Pollard's "Structure and Stress: Social Change among the Fort Sill Apache and Their Ancestors" [165] presents a comprehensive study of acculturation and development.

The Mescalero Apaches by Charles L. Sonnichsen [185], though primarily a history, includes a good deal of ethnographic information. Similarly, T. T. McCord's "An Economic History of the Mescalero Apache" [118] includes material on this group's aboriginal way of life, though the work is primarily an economic history and a study of economic development. Harry W. Basehart's "Mescalero Apache Band Organization and Leadership" [14] has been termed "a work which employs the results of exacting documentary scholarship to reveal important principles of social organization, but, the article suffers from an overabundance of sociological terms. Basehart's "Mescalero Apache Subsistence Patterns and Socio-Political Organization" [203], a Claims Commission paper, includes similar ethnographic material minus the distracting jargon.

Alfred B. Thomas's "The Mescalero Apache" [215] and Averam Bender's "A Study of the Mescalero Apache Indians" [205] include some ethnographic information, though they are primarily historical studies sparked by the Indian Claims Commission. Opler's "Lipan and Mescalero Apache in Texas" [211], a paper presented for the petitioners before the Indian Claims Commission, includes general ethnographic considerations. Given the authority of Opler, this piece must be regarded as an important summary statement of both cultures. His "Mescalero Apache History in the Southwest," written with Catherine H. Opler [161], is a general history of this group based largely upon official sources.

Eastern Apachean Ethnography

"A Summary of Jicarilla Apache Culture," also by

Opler [135], provides an overview of the tribal ethos. As an introductory piece it fulfills its purpose, though a more elaborate study would certainly be welcome. Opler's "Jicarilla Apache Territory, Economy, and Society in 1850" [158] presents some of the same ethnographic data, but emphasizes the extent of Jicarilla territory about 1850, social structure, and especially agricultural practices. This piece clarifies the role of agriculture in Apachean life and implicitly studies economic and political development. H. Clyde Wilson's "Jicarilla Apache Political and Economic Structures" [219] is another impressive study of Jicarilla political and economic development. Dolores A. Gunnerson's *The Jicarilla Apaches* [89], based largely on Spanish documents, reconstructs the history of this Apachean group, emphasizing the elements of adaptability and flexibility. Veronica Tiller's dissertation, "The History of the Jicarilla Apache Tribe" [199], is a compilation of many sources and promises to become an important reference. Tiller is the first Jicarilla to receive the Ph.D. degree. Opler's *Childhood and Youth in Jicarilla Apache Society* [148] follows the life cycle of an individual to the point of marriage and is thus a study of child development within the context of aboriginal Jicarilla culture. "Rule and Practice in the Behavior between Jicarilla Affinal Relatives," also by Opler [134], is a brief, narrowly defined study of social relationships, and his "Pots, Apache, and the Dismal River Culture Aspect" [159] considers Jicarilla pottery in terms of recent archeological research. In the latter article Opler contends that the Dismal River culture, that is, Athapascan sites on the Plains, represents a Pueblo retrenchment.

Several papers generated by the Indian Claims Commission treat Jicarilla ethnography. "Environment, Settlement, and Land Use in the Jicarilla Apache Claim Area," by Burton Le Roy Gordon [208] studies the physical environment of the area along with Jicarilla land use, settlement, and commerce and implicitly concerns the monetary value of the Jicarillas' land. Alfred B. Thomas's "The Jicarilla Apache Indians: A History" [214] includes ethnological items such as agricultural practices and religion, and Jean W. Nelson's "Anthropological Material on the Jicarilla Apaches" [210] summarizes the scholarly literature. "The Jicarilla Apaches," by Elizabeth V. Atwater [202], outlines their way of life during the Spanish-Mexican period. Based upon a painstaking use of early sources, this piece is an important contribution.

The Kiowa Apaches are a much misunderstood group of Indians. The literature on this tribal group is minuscule, even when compared with the others, and most of it concerns their identity. Charles S. Brant's "The Kiowa Apache Indians" [33] and William E. Bittle's "The Position of Kiowa-Apache in the Apachean Group" [24] come to grips with the identity question. Both dissertations conclude that the Kiowa Apaches form a part of the Apachean group regardless of their association with the Kiowa. Bittle's work proceeds by way of a detailed linguistic analysis, whereas Brant focuses on ethnological considerations and issues of acculturation. In addition, Brant has published two articles that conclusively argue the identity question: "The Cultural Position of the Kiowa-Apache" [31] and "Kiowa Apache Culture History" [34]. Serious study of the Kiowa Apaches did not begin until 1933, when J. Gilbert McAllister arrived among them with his notebook. The result, "Kiowa-Apache Social Organization" [117], has become a standard ethnography. It considers both behavior patterns and the life cycle.

Relatively little work has been done among the Lipan Apaches. As of the 1930s, the period of energetic fieldwork, only a few Lipan Apaches had managed to survive, and this remnant had been absorbed by the Mescaleros. A basic source concerning Lipan history and ethnography is Andrée F. Sjoberg's "Lipan Apache Culture in Historical Perspective" [180]. Other fruitful sources of Lipan ethnography are F. M. Buckelew's autobiographies, *Buckelew, the Indian Captive* [9], ed. Seth Barnes, and *Life of F. M. Buckelew, the Indian Captive, as Related by Himself* [37], grounded upon his eleven-month captivity among the Lipans in about 1866. Opler's "Lipan and Mescalero Apache in Texas" [211], though primarily prepared for the Indian Claims Commission, includes a significant summary of Lipan ethnography.

In addition, Opler has written several articles that deal primarily with anthropological theory, though they are actually based upon and refer to his work among both the Eastern and Western Apaches. His "Themes as

Dynamic Forces in Culture" [147] grapples with the issue of cultural patterns and offers clues to the internal dynamic. It also addresses the issue of acculturation. In this piece Opler utilizes Chiricahua and Jicarilla materials. "An Interpretation of Ambivalence of Two American Indian Tribes" [132], a brief early piece, applies the Freudian concept of ambivalence to the Apachean attitudes toward death and dying. Opler argues that psychoanalytic concepts, not derived from the actual life experiences of a people, are not appropriate for anthropological research, though he does not seem willing to press his point. "The Kinship Systems of the Southern Athabaskan-Speaking Tribes" [133], an important article, classifies Apachean kinship systems as belonging to either the Chiricahua or the Jicarilla pattern. This article also addresses the issue of diffusion and the relationships between the different Apachean groups.

Basic Historical Materials

Historical materials, though mainly of the "chasing Geronimo" variety, are much more plentiful than ethnographic texts. This part of the essay deals with general works and those that particularly relate to the Spanish-Mexican and American eras in the Southwest.

As a treaty commissioner once said: "They [Indian children] will only know the history of the fathers by a tradition and the history of the White man's books."

Tragically, these words were an accurate prophecy. The white man's books largely reflect the perspective of a conqueror, and in fact the majority of the relevant historical works deal mainly with military matters. As a result, much of the native American tradition and experience has been lost, never to be regained — not only for the white man, but also for the modern Indian.

On the whole, American historians have tended to ignore the native Americans. They form a minuscule portion of what is essentially the white man's story — the glorious march from sea to shining sea — and in this light are usually treated as a minor hindrance. The Indians, however, had their own rich traditions, passed down in an oral history. Such oral traditions represent their story as they perceive(d) it. Jason Betzinez's *I Fought with Geronimo* [23] and James Kaywaykla's *In the Days of Victorio* [107], among other primary works, embody part of the Apaches' story.

General Works

Thomas E. Mails's *The People Called Apache* [119] serves as an adequate (though barely so) introduction to Apachean history. Frank C. Lockwood's *The Apache Indians* [112] fulfills this same function but in a much more comprehensive manner. Some of Lockwood's material, however, has been superseded by more recent research. John Upton Terrell's *Apache Chronicle* [191] also serves an introductory function, though it is much more detailed than the other two works. Terrell, however, has a penchant for polemical analysis and argumentation, and his work has been challenged as shallow in the native American press.

The Spanish-Mexican Period

The Spaniards consistently viewed the Southwest as a storehouse of treasures. Mesmerized by delusions of instant riches, they eagerly undertook its exploration. Herbert E. Bolton's *Spanish Exploration in the Southwest* [26] contains the accounts of early explorers like Oñate. Donald E. Worcester's "Early Spanish Accounts of the Apache Indians" [222] and Daniel S. Matson's and Albert H. Schroeder's "Cordero's Description of the Apache — 1796" [121] are adequate examples of the value of early relations.

Jack D. Forbes's *Apache, Navaho, and Spaniard* [72] has been recognized as a standard source for early Apachean history. It clearly delineates the pattern in the relationships between the Apaches, other Indian groups, and the Spanish Empire. The value of Forbes's well-documented work is enhanced by his use of Mexican and Spanish archival materials. More narrowly focused studies of these same areas are represented by Forbes's "The Early Western Apache" [73] and William E. Dunn's "Apache Relations in Texas, 1718–1750" [65]. A similar specialized work, actually a case study, is Max L. Moorehead's *The Apache Frontier* [125]. Several Indian Claims Commission papers deal with the Spanish-Mexican period. Included among these are Alfred B. Thomas's

"The Jicarilla Apache Indians: A History, 1598–1888" [214] and his "The Mescalero Apache, 1653–1874" [215], as well as Verne F. Ray's "Ethnohistorical Analysis of Documents Relating to the Apache Indians of Texas" [212]. These particular essays, like the other Indian Claims Commission papers, rely upon primary source materials and are well documented. Ray's paper focuses primarily upon the American period.

During this early period of culture contact the Southwestern Indians were introduced to the horse and the gun, both of which introduced many changes into their way of life. The concepts developed by Frank Secoy in his "Changing Military Patterns on the Great Plains" [179] are important for developing an understanding of the effect of the horse and the gun on Apachean culture. According to Secoy, the Southwestern tribes developed a post-horse but pre-gun culture. This development, in turn, reflected the exigencies of Spanish policy. Frank G. Roe, *The Indian and the Horse* [172], contains the most basic study of the influence of the horse upon native American cultures. A more particular study of both the source of the Indians' horses and the distribution pattern established through trading and raiding is Donald E. Worcester's "The Spread of Spanish Horses in the Southwest, 1700–1800" [223]. La Verne Harrell Clark, *They Sang for Horses* [40], is a study of the changes in Navaho and Apachean folklore and mythology that resulted from the acquisition of the horse.

Official Spanish policy vacillated throughout this era, and wars of extermination alternated with periods of peace. Overall, however, immediate self-interest was the norm for both groups. Ironically, the Apaches and the Spaniards entered an asymmetrical relationship as the Apaches began to develop a dependence upon raiding to supply their needs. Similarly, the businesses associated with frontier military posts were often essential features of territorial economics. Donald E. Worcester's "The Beginnings of the Apache Menace of the Southwest" [221] demonstrates, contrary to Bancroft, that hostilities between the Spaniards and the Apaches originated with the first penetration of the area. The notorious business of scalp-hunting, genocidal in its effect, is described and analyzed in Ralph A. Smith's "The Scalp Hunt in Chihuahua — 1849" [183]. Scalp-hunting, it seems, provided a profitable interlude for California-bound forty-niners. At one time, the state of Sonora paid one hundred and fifty pesos for the scalp of an adult Indian male, fifty for that of a female, and twenty-five for that of a child.

The American Period

Two previously cited works deal most adequately with the American period in the Southwest: Terrell's *Apache Chronicle* [191] and Lockwood's *The Apache Indians* [112]. Bertha Blount's "The Apache in the Southwest" [25], an article based on her thesis at the University of California, contains a synopsis of the important events of this period, as does Douglas Martin's *An Arizona Chronology* [120]. Of the two, Martin presents the more inclusive listing, though both pieces provide a valuable overview. Ralph Ogle's *Federal Control of the Western Apaches, 1848–1886* [129], a frequently cited work, is a well-researched analysis of American and Western Apache relations from the Treaty of Guadalupe-Hidalgo until the final surrender of Geronimo. Originally published as a series of articles in the *New Mexico Historical Review*, this collection has become a basic source since its printing in book form.

Hubert Howe Bancroft's *History of Arizona and New Mexico, 1530–1888* [7] and his *History of Texas and the North Mexican States* [8], though old, contain a wide-ranging history of Arizona, New Mexico, and Texas, focusing in part upon the original inhabitants. Bancroft draws heavily on the old accounts for his treatment of the Spanish period. Frank C. Lockwood's *Pioneer Days in Arizona* [111] contains a basic history of the territory that focuses especially on the hardships involved in advancing civilization. Odie B. Faulk's *Arizona* [68] presents a brief history of the state, while LaFarge's *Santa Fe* [108], taken from the *New Mexican*, describes early Southwestern life. *William Sanders Oury*, a recent biography by his great-grandson, Cornelius C. Smith [182], paints a picture of the Southwest and one of its more notable citizens. Smith's biography, really a genteel work of family history, is especially interesting in regard to Oury's feelings about his role in the Camp Grant massacre. Author Smith defends his great-grandfather by means of a lapse into moral relativism. Similar pieces of local color include John Spring, *John Spring's Arizona* [187], and Will C. Barnes's *Apaches and Longhorns* [11]. The settlers expected the military to protect them against the cunning Apaches — often an impossible task. Richard N. Ellis's "The Apache Chronicle" [66] reprints a sarcastic broadside that appeared in 1880 in the Mesilla Valley of New Mexico. Ellis places the chronicle within the context of contemporary newspaper accounts. This piece mocks the military for their inability to defeat Victorio. In a much more serious vein, the *Memorial and Affidavits Showing Outrages Perpetrated by the Apache Indians* [4] contains the views of the legislature on the ongoing "savage war." This piece, sparked by fear that some of the troops in Arizona territory would be withdrawn, embodies a sense of trepidation — if not desperation. The *Resolution Adopted at Meeting of Residents of Cochise County* [46] embodies a similar tone. Sharlot M. Hall's "Olive A. Oatman" [92], a captivity piece, reports the tragic story of the bloody demise of the Oatman family at the hands of the Apaches. This piece serves to make concrete the complaints of the legislature, and the sarcasm of "The Apache Chronicle". Frank C. Lockwood's *Arizona Characters* [110] and his *More Arizona Characters* [114] present the frontier types in a sympathetic fashion.

As previously remarked, many of the extant historical sources deal primarily with military affairs. Besides various tales of ineptitude, such as Lieutenant Bascom's treatment of Cochise, the theme of this part of the story centers on the white man's frustration. Excellent warriors, ever cunning, the Apaches were more than a match for the military. Never actually conquered, they were really defeated by the Apache Scouts, a group favored by General Crook. The scouts could track and engage hostile groups in their most secret retreats, including the otherwise impenetrable Sierra Madre. A basic source concerning the work of the scouts is Dan L. Thrapp's *Al Sieber, Chief of Scouts* [193]. This book also contains a history of central Arizona, especially the Prescott area.

The foremost contemporary historian of the Southwest is Dan L. Thrapp. Recently retired in the Tucson area after his career with the *Los Angeles Times*, Thrapp has written several justly praised histories of the Southwest. *The Conquest of Apacheria* [194] is his most basic work. As Thrapp notes in his introduction, "Arizona was thought to be rich in minerals, and where wealth lay, white men would go, even if they were forced to fight the most implacable savages on the American continent to get there. Fight them they and the soldiers did, and this book is the story of that long and varied war." The importance of this work rests on its general treatment of the flow of events upon the basis of a firm grasp of details. Thrapp's *Victorio and the Mimbres Apaches* [197] contains a history of this Apachean group as well as a biography of Victorio. Like *The Conquest of Apacheria, Victorio and the Mimbres Apaches* is an outstanding piece of research. This book, like the others by Thrapp, addresses itself to many persistent issues of Southwestern historiography, such as the dispute over the nationality of Victorio. Thrapp's sympathy for the plight of Victorio and the Mimbres and his admiration for Victorio's grasp of military tactics add a sensitivity to the work that only enhances its power. His "Juh: An Incredible Indian" [196] presents a brief biography of Juh, though *Victorio and the Mimbres Apaches* contains a much more comprehensive account that covers much of the same period and similar events. Thrapp's *General Crook and the Sierra Madre Adventure* [195] treats the causal interrelationship between the Cibecue affair, a seemingly minor event, the Chiricahua outbreak from San Carlos, and the resulting expedition into the Sierra Madre under General Crook. "A Man Called Geronimo," also by Thrapp [198], presents a general biography of this notable warrior written for a general audience. Jason Betzinez, "the literate and honest Apache" [197, p. 7], in his *I Fought with Geronimo* [23] includes a good deal of relevant material. *Geronimo's Story of His Life* [13], edited by S. M. Barrett, and James Kaywaykla's *In the Days of Victorio* [107] are other primary sources. The Geronimo volume, however, can be accepted only with grave reservations. Kaywaykla's "I Survived the Massacre of Tres Castillos" [105], specifically descriptive of this battle, is also incorporated within and is a natural conclusion to his *In the Days of Victorio*. Several Indian Claims Commission papers present well-documented accounts of the relations between the Apaches and the Americans. Besides those already mentioned, these include Kenneth Neighbours's "Government, Land, and Indian Policies Relative to Lipan, Mescalero, and Tigua Indians" [209], Averam Bender's "A Study of Western Apache Indians, 1846–1886" [206], Donald Cutter's "Indian Land Rights in the Jicarilla Apache Area" [207], and Bender's "A Study of the Jicarilla

Apache Indians" [204]. These pieces tend to focus on the issues of territorial control and land use.

The Bascom Affair: A Case Study

Typically in Southwestern historiography, sources contradict each other and critically important documents cannot now be located. An example is the Bascom affair, which touched off an Apache war. In brief, a band of Pinal Apaches raided the ranch of a man named John Ward in October, 1860. Ward, however, became convinced that they were members of Cochise's band of Chiricahuas. When Lieutenant George Bascom investigated the affair he seized Cochise, but the chief escaped and began hostilities that lasted for twelve years.

Lt. Bascom filed reports justifying his conduct and was promoted to captain within a year. Robert M. Utley, in "The Bascom Affair: A Reconstruction" [216], marshals a great deal of evidence at variance with Bascom's accounts, and Benjamin H. Sacks, in "New Evidence on the Bascom Affair" [173] offers another reconstruction. Though writers now agree on the main outline of the events, details still vary tremendously, and reconstructions can be varied even further by collating data from such authors as Terrell, Lockwood, and Thrapp. As Utley notes, "that no two chroniclers agree on what happened stems largely from the scarcity of original source material, and from the fact that the few participants who did leave testimony themselves disagreed."

Military Affairs

Most of the literature regarding the Apaches concerns military affairs. In addition to previously cited
works, especially those by Thrapp, John G. Bourke's *On
the Border with Crook* [29] is justly regarded as an authoritative basic source of Southwestern history. Bourke
served on General Crook's staff for sixteen years and was
one of the first serious ethnologists working among the
Apaches. His colorful account is also anecdotal and includes many items of general Southwestern history. His
An Apache Campaign in the Sierra Madre [28] is the accepted work concerning Crook's penetration of the
Sierra Madre. Bourke's notebooks [27] have been published in volumes 8 through 13 of the *New Mexico Historical Review* under the title "Bourke on the Southwest".
James H. Tevis's *Arizona in the '50's* [192] must also be
regarded as a basic source, especially for incidents involv-
ing the Chiricahuas. Tevis was the agent at the stage-
coach station in Apache Pass. According to Thrapp, "the
Tevis narrative is of interest and he presents many novel
and perhaps true incidents of life among the Chiricahuas
[197, p. 335, n. 8].

A variety of pieces deal with particular incidents such
as the Bascom affair. James M. Barney's "The Battle of
Apache Pass" [12] portrays the California column and its
struggle at the pass. In fact, owing to the terror associated
with Apache Pass several articles deal with the various
battles that occurred there. R. A. Mulligan's "Apache
Pass and Old Fort Bowie" [126] provides a general

treatment of some of the more horrendous moments in the pass as well as a history of Fort Bowie. Apache Pass was the primary route west because of its unfailing supply of spring water, and Fort Bowie was established to control this source of water. Similar articles are Fenton Taylor's "The West's Bloodiest Pass" [190] and Barbara Ann Tyler's "Cochise: Apache War Leader, 1858–1861" [200], though the latter article is more general in scope than the previously mentioned ones. The Camp Grant massacre, "the bloodiest page in the Angle-Saxon records of Arizona [112, p. 178], occurred on 30 April 1871. At dawn a group of Americans, Mexicans, and Papago Indians descended upon a large group of Apaches who had sought refuge at Camp Grant. Butchery was the order of the day, and few of those in the encampment were spared, regardless of age or sex. The accounts of this massacre, much like those of the Bascom affair, are extremely confused and contradictory. Was Lieutenant Whitman, the officer who granted the Apaches sanctuary, a crazed drunkard who was harboring murdering and thieving savages, or did a band of white savages with their Indian allies descend upon peacefully sleeping Apaches? According to the official record the white men and their allies were found innocent by a jury of their peers. Yet the trial took place only when President Grant threatened to place the entire territory under martial law. The general histories usually deal with this massacre. For example, John Upton Terrell, in *Apache Chronicle* [191], sketches a bleak design of the white man's actions. Don Schellie's *Vast Domain of Blood* [176] presents a history of the Camp Grant massacre and the resulting trial of the participants. According to Terrell, this book is outstanding. Vincent Colyer's *Peace with the Apaches of New Mexico and Arizona* [48] compiles a great deal of material relating to the massacre, including sworn statements by those familiar with the overall situation. Colyer, on the whole, is supportive of Whitman, as is Terrell in his *Apache Chronicle.* Frank C. Lockwood's "Cochise, the Noble Warrior" [113] considers the Bascom affair and the Cochise-Jeffords relationship within the context of a general overview. "The Apaches' Last Stand in Arizona," by Will C. Barnes [10], describes the battle of the Big Dry Wash. It includes accounts never previously published. Lee Myers's "The Enigma of Mangas Coloradas' Death" [127] recounts and evaluates the various tales of this murder. King Woolsey's bloody career is treated by Clara T. Woody in "The Woolsey Expeditions of 1864" [220]. Woolsey, according to some accounts, reputedly poisoned Indians during the notorious Pinole Treaty. According to Thrapp, Woody is the "historian unrivaled of central Arizona" [193, p. ix]. She provides information that implicitly supports the bleakest interpretations of the Pinole Treaty. The Cibecue battle is treated within the context of the concentration policy by Ralph H. Ogle in "The Apache and the Government" [128]. Paul Schliesser's "The Apache Mutiny of 1881" [177] also deals with the Cibecue affair, but in a human-interest fashion. Yet few of these articles provide a concise overview, and they are used most fruitfully in combination with several of the general histories.

Stories of "chasing Geronimo" are voluminous in Southwestern history. Primary among these are *Geronimo's Story of His Life*, edited by S. M. Barrett [13], and *I Fought with Geronimo* [23] by Jason Betzinez with Wilbur S. Nye. Dan Thrapp, as previously remarked, is generally accepted as the primary commentator, and he treats most of the other primary and secondary accounts in his various books. His comments are reliable. Several pieces by other authors, however, demand special note. Gustave Fiebeger's "General Crook's Campaign in Old Mexico in 1883" [70] embodies the point of view of a participant. Actually, this piece is more general than the title suggests. Fiebeger served as General George Crook's engineering officer and traveled with the general to meet with Torres and others in Mexico. General Crook's report upon assuming command in the Department of Arizona, *Report on the Apaches* [52], provides essential information. Crook's sympathy for the plight of the Apaches is especially interesting in light of his reputation as their implacable foe. Similarly, his Annual Report for 1885 [53] considers the outbreak of Geronimo, the issue of tiswin drinking, and the problems resulting from the division of authority between the War Department and the Department of the Interior. Crook's concern for justice for the Apaches is demonstrated by his *Resume of Operations against Apache Indians, 1882–1886* [54]. His autobiography, *General George Crook* [55], contains a good deal of material on the Geronimo wars as well as a report of his efforts to have the Chiricahuas removed from Florida. General Nelson A. Miles's *Personal Recollections and Observations* [124] presents material relating to the close of the wars. Miles, however, refused to credit Gatewood's role in the surrender. "Lieutenant Charles B. Gatewood and the Surrender of Geronimo" [75] corrects Miles's *Recollections*. General Oliver O. Howard's *My Life and Experiences among Our Hostile Indians* [100] contains material relating to the Howard-Cochise Treaty. Crook complained that he could not discover its terms, even though he was the commanding general in the department. The treaty itself was an oral agreement between Howard and Cochise, and it was never published. The issue is whether or not General Howard tacitly acknowledged the right of the Chiricahuas to raid into Mexico. According to Eve Ball, Britton Davis's *The Truth about Geronimo* [57], a military history, is considered authentic by the Apaches, whereas Anton Mazzanovich's *Trailing Geronimo* [122] is not [107, pp. 212-13].

The Reservation Period

Reservation life is portrayed in Robert Frazer's *The Apaches of the White Mountain Reservation* [74]. Frazer accompanied General Crook on a visit to the reservation in about 1883.

John Clum's biography *Apache Agent* [43], written by Woodworth Clum, provides much information concerning his tenure as agent at San Carlos as well as pertinent historical material, such as the tragic story of Juan José.

An apologia for Clum's career and views, the book details his turbulent days among the Apaches. Testy by nature, and never a friend of the military, Clum was certainly a colorful character. His "Gerónimo" [41], published in several issues of the *New Mexico Historical Review*, covers the career of the cunning warrior, among other things; but it is more important for its presentation of Clum's own views. As a historical piece it is not especially accurate. Clum's "Apache Misrule: A Bungling Agent Sets the Military Arm in Motion" [42] represents him at his apologetic and polemical best.

The Way of the Apaches

The Apaches formed a cosmological society. For them the cosmos, a shining thing, embodied the divine totality. Usually pictured as layered, it had a top and a bottom, and everything was enclosed within it. All was immanent; the cosmos was tensionally closed. Order existed from the mythic time of the beginnings; the parts existed in a relationship ordained by the will, speech, and actions of the cosmogonic gods. This is the case with the Memphite Theology and Maka's Story, the Lakota cosmogony, as well as the Apachean moccasin game. But as opposed to ancient Egypt and Mesopotamia, the Apaches formed a cosmological gens, not an empire.

Owing to the work of scholars like Mircea Eliade and Henri Frankfort it is now generally accepted that the myths of cosmological societies must be taken seriously if such cultures are to be understood in other than ideological guises. Myths, says Eliade, are epiphanic; they describe the intersection of the sacred with the profane.

> Myth narrates a sacred history; it relates an event that took place in primordial time, the fabled time of "beginnings." In other words, myth tells how, through the deeds of supernatural beings, a reality came into existence, be it the whole of reality, the Cosmos, or only a fragment of reality—an island, a species of plant, a particular kind of human behavior, an institution. Myth, then, is always an account of a "creation"; it relates how something was produced, began to *be*. Myth tells only of that which *really* happened, which manifested itself completely. The actors in myths are Supernatural beings. They are known primarily by what they did in the transcendant times of the "beginnings." Hence myths disclose their creative activity and reveal the sacredness (or simply the "supernaturalness") of their works. In short, myths describe the various and sometimes dramatic breakthroughs of the sacred (or the "supernatural") into the world. [Mircea Eliade, *Myth and Reality*, trans. Willard Trask (New York: Harper and Row, 1963), pp. 5–6.]

Given this understanding, the Chiricahua creation story is a myth, as are the cosmogonies of Genesis. Tales and fables, on the other hand, can and do describe the origin and changes of men and things, but they do not explain the fundament of the human condition. In this sense, the ancient Epic of Gilgamesh is a myth that deals with the origin and necessity of death, while the folktale of Little

Red Riding Hood seems merely to be a tale about the need for prudence when walking through woods to visit grandmothers. Myths, to put it another way, deal with the primordial events that constitute man existentially — that define his condition and the world in which he discovers himself.

The events of the beginnings are also "exemplary models for all human rites and all significant human activities" (Eliade, p. 8). Myth is thus linked to ritual. This can be discerned in the Chiricahua moccasin game. Usually understood and often summarily treated as a gambling contest, the moccasin game clearly represents the People's participation in the life-giving cycle of the cosmos. It recreates the primal contest that, through the victory of the winged creatures, led to the establishment of day. More important, owing to this victory of the winged creatures man can exist. Interestingly enough, the moccasin game is a non-zero-sum game of chance, not a game of skill. In playing the game the People recreate and participate in the triumph of the winged creatures, which is also a victory for man, a victory of life over darkness. This linkage points to a fundamental difference in the understanding of time. The modern conception is that time is linear and that it moves toward an end that is usually considered to be civilizational achievement or progress. Though the past is the prologue of the future, time itself is not reversible. To the mythic mind, however, time, like reality itself, is conceived of as layered. Through ritual an individual can enter sacred time, the fecund time of the beginnings.

Thus, the Chiricahuas lived not only in linear time (represented by counting years, if only in terms of the age of individuals), but also in sacred or primal time, as through the moccasin game.

Mythology

The current anthropological literature on Apachean mythology is somewhat flawed. Many anthropologists, it seems, labor under positivistic biases that preclude a genuine understanding of myth. With the exception of some of Opler's work, their interest in myth centers mainly on issues of diffusion and linguistics.

The approach of early ethnographers and anthropologists is typically marked by an attempt to locate the Indians' place upon the great ladder of progress. Just what stage of civilization have they achieved? The implicit assumption is that of engineering; if one can discover a people's position upon the ladder one can, with enough study and knowledge, induce the conditions that can propel them upward toward the higher levels.

Several articles, monographs, and books deal with Apachean mythology and folklore materials. These works usually include a general ethnographic introduction and linguistic notes, and they constitute the basic research tools in this area. Included among these are Morris E. Opler's *Myths and Tales of the Chiricahua Apache Indians* [143], *Myths and Tales of the Jicarilla Indians* [136], and *Myths and Legends of the Lipan Apache Indians* [139]; Pliny E. Goddard's "Jicarilla Apache Texts" [78], "San

Carlos Apache Texts" [80], and "White Mountain Apache Texts" [81]; and Harry Hoijer's *Chiricahua and Mescalero Apache Texts* [95]. The previously cited primary ethnological works also include relevant information — for example, Opler's *An Apache Life-Way* [141] and James Kaywaykla's *In the Days of Victorio* [107].

Religion

Apachean religion expresses the relationship between the People and their gods. Contrary to the popular misunderstanding, the Apaches, like other cosmological peoples, were especially religious. In fact, their way of life was marked by piety and by imitation of the patterns of action established by the cosmogonic gods in the time of the beginnings. For example, during the warrior training of the Chiricahua novice he was called Child of the Water (the name of the divine culture hero).

Once again the primary ethnological sources are relevant, especially Betzinez and Nye's *I Fought With Geronimo* [23] and Kaywaykla's *In the Days of Victorio* [107]. Opler's *An Apache Life-Way* [141] and John G. Bourke's "The Medicine-Men of the Apache" [30], recently reprinted, are the most important secondary accounts. Bourke's work is of special note for his extensive treatment of the use of pollen.

Many articles, especially those by Opler, deal with Apachean religion, but few deal adequately with the subject, given the understanding of religion discovered in the field of comparative religion. For the Apaches, the cosmos was pervaded by both benign and malevolent forces, and this same emphasis is discovered in Apachean mythology. Studies of Apachean witchcraft focus on the role of the malevolent forces in the Apachean lifeway. Keith H. Basso's *Western Apache Witchcraft* [17] and Opler's *An Apache Life-Way* [141], in conjunction with his "Notes on Chiricahua Apache Culture" [153], contain basic information. Opler's "The Concept of Supernatural Power among the Chiricahua and Mescalero Apaches" [130] presents the situation in a very clear, concise manner, as does his "Chiricahua Apache Material Relating to Sorcery" [149]. Grenville Goodwin's "White Mountain Apache Religion" [84] furnishes a general outline.

The role of the shaman within Apachean religion is dealt with in John G. Bourke's "The Medicine-Men of the Apache" [30] and Opler's *An Apache Life-Way* [141]. More specialized pieces include Opler's "The Creative Role of Shamanism in Mescalero Apache Mythology" [150] and his "Remuneration to Supernaturals and Man in Apachean Ceremonialism" [156].

The Mountain Spirits represent beneficent power; they preserve and protect the people. Besides primary source materials, brief, summary articles on this include M. R. Harrington's "The Devil Dance of the Apache" [93] and Opler's "Mountain Spirits of the Chiricahua" [151] and his "The Sacred Clowns of the Chiricahua and Mescalero Indians" [137]. These articles, however, tend to repeat information available in the primary and more important secondary sources.

The issue of acculturation is implicitly considered in Opler's "The Use of Peyote by the Carrizo and Lipan Apache Tribes" [138] and in Charles S. Brant's "Peyotism among the Kiowa-Apache and Neighboring Tribes" [32], while a native apocalyptic movement is treated in Grenville Goodwin and Charles Kaunt's "A Native Religious Movement among the White Mountain and Cibecue Apache" [88]. Goodwin's "Comparison of Navaho and White Mountain Apache Ceremonial Forms and Categories" [86] studies diffusion. A series of articles that discusses the Apachean reaction to death and dying includes Opler's "Reaction to Death among the Mescalero Apache" [152], "The Death Practices and Eschatology of the Kiowa Apache" (with William E. Bittle) [160], "The Lipan Apache Death Complex and Its Extensions" [146], and "Myth and Practice in Jicarilla Apache Eschatology" [155], the most insightful piece in this group.

Ritual

The Apaches have a dramatic, almost Manichean conception of the cosmos, emphasizing the struggle between beneficent and malevolent powers on both a cosmic and a mundane level. The first moccasin game embodies the cosmic struggle, while the coyote cycle represents the cosmic struggle transferred to earth. Anthropologists, on the whole, appear to lack the training in comparative religion that would enable them to understand cosmological ritual in its proper context. For example, Opler's informants make it clear that the pubescent girl *is* White Painted Woman during the puberty ceremony. Opler, following anthropological principles that are implicitly ethnocentric, chooses to apply different terms to the relationship. This confusion is grounded in the scholarly literature, and by way of the standard ethnographies it is transferred to the popular literature, as in Thomas E. Mails's *The People Called Apache* [119], for example.

Besides primary works and the more important secondary pieces, several articles deal with Apachean ritual. Most of these articles, however, treat either the girl's puberty ceremony or the Masked Dancer complex. Articles dealing with the puberty ceremony include Byron Cummings's "Apache Puberty Ceremony for Girls" [56] and Opler's "Adolescence Rite of the Jicarilla" [142]. The Masked Dancers are treated in Pliny E. Goddard's "The Masked Dancers of the Apache" [79], M. R. Harrington's "The Devil Dance of the Apache" [93], Henry Kane's "The Apache Secret Devil Dance" [104], Opler's "Mountain Spirits of the Chiricahua" [151], and Clara Lee Tanner's "Spirits Which Come out of the Mountains" [189]. Tanner's short piece is especially interesting in that she explicitly identifies the pubescent girl as White Painted Woman. These articles, however, repeat a great deal of the same information. An overview is provided by Opler's *An Apache Life-Way* [141], John G. Bourke's "The Medicine-Men of the Apache" [30], and Keith H. Basso's "The Gift of Changing Woman" [15]. Opler and Hoijer study the novice's war training in their

"The Raid and War-Path Language of the Chiricahua Apache" [140]. More detailed and narrowly focused studies include Opler's "The Character and Derivation of the Jicarilla Holiness Rite" [144] and his "Childhood and Youth in Jicarilla Apache Society [148]. Both of these pieces include the relevant mythological material. Studies of diffusion include Opler's "Navaho Shamanistic Practice among the Jicarilla Apache" [145] and his "The Influence of Aboriginal Pattern and White Contact on a Recently Introduced Ceremony, the Mescalero Peyote Rite" [131].

As previously remarked, mythology, ritual, and religion interpenetrate to provide an understanding of the Apachean way of life. To put it another way, the moccasin game is not a mere gambling contest, but is the ritual participation of the People in the victory of the winged creatures over the beasts. Michael E. Melody's "The Sacred Hoop" [123] deals with the intersection of mythology, religion, and ritual so as to illuminate the Chiricahuas' way of life and their form of government.

Ethnographic Notes

Art and Basketry

Besides brief notes such as K. T. Dodge's "White Mountain Apache Baskets" [58], very little work has been done in the area of art and basketry. Dorothy Frances Gay's "Apache Art" [76], though finished before Opler's research was readily available, is a credible piece of work.

The aim of this thesis is to present the distinctive features of Apachean art. An account designed as a museum guide is Frederic H. Douglas's *Apache Baskets* [59]. "Basketry of the San Carlos Apache," by Helen H. Roberts [171], is the most scholarly and comprehensive work in this area.

Costume

The *Material Culture Notes* issued by the Denver Art Museum contain relevant pieces. Included among these are Frederic H. Douglas's "A Jicarilla Apache Beaded Cape" [60]. "A Jicarilla Apache Woman's Skin Dress" [62], and "A Jicarilla Apache Man's Skin Leggings" [61]. Charles F. Lummis contributes "Chiricahua Apache Costume in the 1880's" [116]. Material can also be found in the primary ethnographies and the important secondary accounts, such as Opler's *An Apache Life-Way* [141].

Government

References to aboriginal Apachean government abound throughout the literature. Opler includes a brief section on this subject at the end of *An Apache Life-Way* [141]. His data, however, are meant to apply to the local group and not to the band level of organization. Harry W. Basehart's "Mescalero Apache Band Organization and Leadership" [14] attempts to outline the principles of government in this Apachean group, but the article suffers from terminological confusion. His "Mescalero Apache Subsistence Patterns and Socio-Political Organization" [203], an Indian Claims Commission paper, is a much more adequate piece of work. Michael E. Melody's "The Sacred Hoop" [123] includes the most elaborate secondary account.

The modern form of government among the Apaches can be discerned in the *Constitution and Bylaws of the Apache Tribe of the Mescalero Reservation* [1], *Corporate Charter of the Apache Tribe of the Mescalero Reservation* [2], *Corporate Charter of the San Carlos Apache Tribe* [175], *Constitution and By-Laws of the San Carlos Apache Tribe* [174], *Constitution and By-Laws of the White Mountain Apache Tribe* [218], *Constitution and By-Laws of the Jicarilla Apache Tribe* [102], and *Corporate Charter of the Jicarilla Apache Tribe* [103]. It appears that the Apaches now understand themselves in the liberal-bourgeois terms of western constitutionalism. More dynamic approaches include Harry T. Getty's "The San Carlos Indian Cattle Industry" [77] and Charles Leland Sonnichsen's *The Mescalero Apaches* [185].

Language and Linguistics

Harry Hoijer's "The Position of the Apachean Language in the Athapaskan Stock" [99] and his "The Southern Athapascan Languages" [96] place the Southern Athapascan dialects within their proper context. A variety of more specialized studies also exist, including Keith H. Basso's "The Western Apache Classificatory Verb System" [16]; Harry Hoijer's "The Structure of the Noun in Apachean Languages" [98]; his "The Apachean

Verb" [97]; Herbert J. Landar's "The Loss of Athapascan Words for Fish in the Southwest" [109], and Opler's "The Raid and War-Path Language of the Chiricahua Apache" [140]. The linguistic notes in the mythological studies also include a good deal of information.

Photographs

C. S. Fly's *Geronimo the Apache* [71] mainly presents a photographic study of this celebrated warrior. On the whole, Fly's work chronicles the turbulent frontier period of Southwestern history. He was well located for this — in Tombstone at the Fremont Street entrance to the OK Corral. His studio is now part of the OK Corral "tourist attraction" in Tombstone. The display includes copies of some of his more notable photographs. Fly, it seems, possessed the verve of the modern newspaper man. Among other things, he witnessed the gunfight at the OK Corral, and he was present during the negotiations with Geronimo in the Canyon de los Embudos.

The Arizona Pioneers' Historical Society (see *A Library of Arizona History* [3]) is the primary depository of Apachean photographs. The society's collections include more than 180,000 items, many of which are identified and classified by subject.

CONCLUSION

"Apache! Apache!" This terror-filled shout is no longer heard in the Southwest except as children use the cry in their more gruesome games. The Apaches, whose cunning and courage once horrified the strongest of men, have been subdued. But the task of understanding them, as the available literature readily demonstrates, has just begun.

The last of the proud and fearsome Chiricahuas are buried at Fort Sill. As the artillery crashes on a nearby test range, one can stand amid their remains. Geronimo is there; his grave, prominent among the others, has been desecrated. With the artillery barrage sounding a dirge, it seems that the army wishes to remind visitors of its victory — one that it never really achieved. Or perhaps it wishes to assure itself that the haughty Chiricahuas have been beaten; that in death they finally did submit.

The sons and daughters of the People live on, on reservations throughout the Southwest. Largely undefeated even by the poverty imposed upon them, they remain proud in their silence.

ALPHABETICAL LIST AND INDEX
*Denotes items suitable for secondary school students.

Item
no.

Essay
page
no.

[1]   Apache Tribe of the Mescalero Reserva-
tion. 1936. *Constitution and By-Laws of the*
Apache Tribe of the Mescalero Reservation,
New Mexico. Approved March 25, 1936.
Washington: U.S. Government Printing
Office.   (52)

[2]   Apache Tribe of the Mescalero Reserva-
tion. 1937. *Corporate Charter of the Apache*
Tribe of the Mescalero Reservation, New
Mexico. Ratified August 1, 1936.
Washington: U.S. Government Printing
Office.   (52)

[3]   American Pioneers' Historical Society.
1966. *A Library of Arizona History: Intro-*
duction and Guide to the Library of the
Arizona Pioneers' Historical Society.
Tucson: Arizona Pioneers' Historical
Society.   (53)

[4]   Arizona (Territory) Legislative Assem-
bly. 1871. *Memorial and Affidavits Showing*
Outrages Perpetrated by the Apache Indians,
in the Territory of Arizona, for the Years 1869

and 1870. San Francisco: Francis and
Valentine, Printers. (33)

[5]* Armstrong, Virginia Irving (comp.).
1971. *I Have Spoken: American History
through the Voices of the Indians.* Chicago:
The Swallow Press. (12)

[6] Baldwin, Gordon. 1965. *The Warrior
Apaches: A Story of the Chiricahua and Western Apache.* Tucson: D. S. King. (19)

[7] Bancroft, Hubert Howe. 1889. *History of
Arizona and New Mexico 1530–1888.* San
Francisco: The History Company. (32)

[8] _____. 1890. *History of Texas and the
North Mexican States.* 2 vols. San Francisco: The History Company. (32)

[9] Banta, Seth E. 1911. *Buckelew, the Indian
Captive.* Mason, Texas: The Mason
Herald. (31)

[10] Barnes, Will C. 1931. "The Apaches'
Last Stand in Arizona, the Battle of the
Big Dry Wash." *Arizona Historical Review*
3:36–59. (39)

[11] Barnes, William C. 1941. *Apaches and
Longhorns: The Reminiscences of Will C.
Barnes,* ed. Frank C. Lockwood. Los
Angeles: Ward Ritchie Press. (33)

[12]* Barney, James M. 1936. "The Battle of Apache Pass." *Arizona Highways* 12, No. 1:10–11, 20–22; 12, No. 2:15, 24. (37)

[13]* Barrett, S. M., ed. 1906. *Geronimo's Story of His Life*. New York: Duffield and Co. (Reprinted as *Geronimo, His Own Story*, ed. Frederick W. Turner III. New York: Dulton, 1970.) (13, 40)

[14] Basehart, Harry W. 1971. "Mescalero Apache Band Organization and Leadership," *Anthropological Papers of the University of Arizona* 21:35–49. (23, 51)

[15] Basso, Keith H. 1966. "The Gift of Changing Woman," Anthropological Papers No. 76, *Bureau of American Ethnology Bulletin* 196:113–173. (49)

[16] ———. 1968. "The Western Apache Classificatory Verb System: A Formal Analysis," *Southwestern Journal of Anthropology* 24:252–266. (52)

[17]* ———. 1968. *Western Apache Witchcraft, Anthropological Papers of the University of Arizona* 15.

[18] ———. 1970. *The Cibecue Apache: Case Studies in Cultural Anthropology*. New York: Holt, Rinehart and Winston. (20)

[19]   ———. 1971. " 'To Give Up on Words':
Silence in Western Apache Culture," *Anthropological Papers on the University of Arizona* 21:151–161.   (20)

[20]*   ———, ed. 1971. *Western Apache Raiding
and Warfare, from the Notes of Grenville
Goodwin*. Tucson: University of Arizona
Press.   (19)

[21]   Beals, Ralph L. 1934. *Material Culture of
the Pima, Papago, and Western Apache, with
Suggestions for Museum Displays. Berkeley:
U.S. National Parks Service*.   (21)

[22]   Bellah, Robert N. 1952. *Apache Kinship
Systems*. Cambridge, Mass.: Harvard
University Press.   (18)

[23]*   Betzinez, Jason, with Wilbur S. Nye.
1959. *I Fought with Geronimo*. Harrisburg,
Pa.: Stackpole Company.   (14, 28)

[24]   Bittle, William E. 1956. "The Position of
Kiowa-Apache in the Apachean Group.
Ph.D. dissertation, University of
California, Los Angeles.   (25)

[25]   Blount, Bertha. 1919. "The Apache in
the Southwest, 1846–1886," *The South-
western Historical Quarterly* 23:20–38.   (31)

[26]   Bolton, Herbert E., ed. 1916. *Spanish Ex-*

ploration in the Southwest, 1542–1706.
New York: Charles Scribner's Sons.   (29)

[27]   Bourke, John G. MSS. notebooks. University of Arizona, Tucson. Partially printed as "Bourke on the Southwest," ed. Lansing B. Bloom, *New Mexico Historical Review* 8(1933):1-30; 9(1934:33-77; 10(1935):1-35; 11(1936):77-122; 12(1937):41-77; 13(1938):192-238.   (37)

[28] *   _____. 1886. *An Apache Campaign in the Sierra Madre.* New York: Charles Scribner's Sons. (Reprinted 1958.)   (37)

[29] *   _____. 1891. *On the Border with Crook.* New York: Charles Scribner's Sons. (Reprinted 1971, Lincoln: University of Nebraska Press.)   (37)

[30] *   _____. 1892. "The Medicine-Men of the Apache." Washington, D.C.: *Annual Report of the Bureau of American Ethnology* 9 (1887–88): 443-603.   (46)

[31]   Brant, Charles S. 1949. "The Cultural Position of the Kiowa-Apache," *Southwestern Journal of Anthropology* 5:56-61.   (11, 26)

[32]   _____. 1950. "Peyotism among the Kiowa-Apache and Neighboring Tribes," *Southwestern Journal of Anthropology* 6:212–222.   (48)

[33]   ———. 1951. "The Kiowa Apache Indians: A Study in Ethnology and Acculturation." Ph.D. dissertation, Cornell University.   (25)

[34]   ———. 1953. "Kiowa Apache Culture History: Some Further Observations," *Southwestern Journal of Anthropology* 9:195–202.   (26)

[35]   ———, ed. 1969. *Jim Whitewolf: The Life of a Kiowa Apache*. New York: Dover Publications.   (15)

[36]   Brown, Dee. 1971. *Bury My Heart at Wounded Knee: An Indian History of the American West*. Holt, Rinehart and Winston.   (12)

[37]   Buckelew, F. M. 1925. *Life of F. M. Buckelew, the Indian Captive, as Related by Himself*, eds. Thomas S. Dennis and Lucy S. Dennis. Bandera, Texas: Hunter's Printing House.   (26)

[38]   Buskirk, Winfred. 1949. "Western Apache Subsistence Economy." Ph.D. dissertation, University of New Mexico.   (21)

[39]   Capps, Inez H. 1952. "Social Change among the White Mountain Apache Indians from the 1880s to the Present." M. A. thesis, Montana State University.   (21)

[40]   Clark, LaVerne Harrell. 1966. *They Sang for Horses; The Impact of the Horse on Navajo and Apache Folklore*. Tucson: University of Arizona Press.   (30)

[41]   Clum, John P. 1928. "Gerónimo," *New Mexico Historical Review* 3:1–41, 121–144, 217–264.   (42)

[42]   ———. 1930. "Apache Misrule: A Bungling Agent Sets the Military Arm in Motion," *New Mexico Historical Review* 5:138–153, 221–239.   (42)

[43]   Clum, Woodworth. 1936. *Apache Agent: The Story of John P. Clum*. Boston: Houghton Mifflin and Co.   (41)

[44]   Cochise, Ciyé. 1971. *The First Hundred Years of Niño Cochise: The Untold Story of an Apache Indian Chief*, ed. A. Kinney Griffith. London: Abelard-Schuman.   (15)

[45]   Cochise, Niño, and A. K. Griffith. 1967. "Apache Tears," *Old West* 4, No. 2, p. 15.   (16)

[46]   [Cochise County, Arizona.] 1885. *Resolution Adopted at Meeting of Residents of Cochise County, Arizona, Regarding Outbreak of Indians from San Carlos Reservation*. Washington, D.C.: T. McGill and Co.   (33)

[47]   Collier, Miles M. 1960. "Apache Laws,"
        True West 6, No. 6, pp. 11, 60.   (18)

[48]   Colyer, Vincent. 1872. *Peace with the
        Apaches of New Mexico and Arizona. United
        States Board of Indian Commissioners Report*
        (1871). Washington, D.C.: Government
        Printing Office.   (39)

[49]   Cremony, John C. 1868. "The Apache
        Race," *The Overland Monthly* 1:201–209.   (16)

[50]*   _____. 1868. *Life among the Apaches*. San
        Francisco: A. Roman and Co. (Reprinted
        1969, Glorieta, New Mexico: Rio Grande
        Press.)   (16)

[51]   _____. 1872. "Some Savages," *The Over-
        land Monthly* 8:201–210.   (16)

[52]   Crook, George. 1883. [Report on the
        Apaches] *To the Adjutant General, Military
        Division of the Pacific*. U.S. Army, De-
        partment of Arizona.   (40)

[53]   _____. 1885. *Annual Report of Brigadier
        General George Crook, U.S. Army, Com-
        manding Department of Arizona*. U.S.
        Army, Department of Arizona.   (40)

[54]   _____. 1886. *Resume of Operations against
        Apache Indians, 1882–1886*. (Reprinted

1971, London: Johnson-Taunton Military Press.) (40)

[55] ———. 1946. *General George Crook, His Autobiography*, ed. Martin F. Schmitt. Norman: University of Oklahoma Press. (40)

[56] Cummings, Byron. 1939. "Apache Puberty Ceremony for Girls," *The Kiva* 5:1–4. (49)

[57] Davis, Britton. 1939. *The Truth About Geronimo*, ed. Milo M. Quaife. New Haven: Yale University Press. (41)

[58] Dodge, K. T. 1900. "White Mountain Apache Baskets," *American Anthropologist* 2:193–194. (50)

[59] Douglas, Frederic H. 1935. *Apache Baskets*. Pasadena: Esto Publishing Co. (51)

[60] ———. 1939. "A Jicarilla Apache Beaded Cape," *Material Culture Notes* 9:34–37. Denver: Denver Art Museum. (51)

[61] ———. 1953. "A Jicarilla Apache Man's Skin Leggings," *Material Culture Notes* 22:102–107. Denver: Denver Art Museum. (51)

[62] ———. 1953. "A Jicarilla Apache Woman's Skin Dress," *Material Culture Notes*

20:92–96. Denver: Denver Art
Museum.   (51)

[63]   Driver, Harold E. 1969. *Indians of North
America*. 2d ed. rev. Chicago: University
of Chicago Press.   (11)

[64]   Dunn, Jacob P., Jr. 1886. *Massacres of the
Mountains: A History of the Indian Wars of
the Far West*. New York: Harper and
Brothers. (Reprinted 1958, New York:
Archer House.)   (12)

[65]   Dunn, William E. 1911. "Apache Relations in Texas, 1718–1750," *Quarterly of
the Texas State Historical Association*
14:198–274.   (29)

[66]   Ellis, Richard N., ed. 1972. " 'The
Apache Chronicle,' " *New Mexico Historical Review* 47:275–282.   (33)

[67]   Everett, Michael W. 1971. "White Moun-
tain Apache Medical Decision-Making,"
*Anthropological Papers of the University of
Arizona* 21:135–150.   (21)

[68]   Faulk, Odie B. 1970. *Arizona: A Short History*. Norman: University of Oklahoma
Press.   (32)

[69] *   Federal Writers' Project, Arizona. "The

Apache," *Arizona State Teachers College Bulletin* 20:1. (17)

[70] Fiebeger, Gustave. 1936. "General Crook's Campaign in Old Mexico in 1883," *Proceedings of the Annual Meeting of the Order of Indian Wars of the United States*, p. 22–32. Washington, D.C. (40)

[71] Fly, C. S. n.d. *Geronimo the Apache*. Tombstone, Arizona. (53)

[72] * Forbes, Jack D. 1960. *Apache, Navaho, and Spaniard*. Norman: University of Oklahoma Press. (2, 29)

[73] ———. 1966. "The Early Western Apache, 1300–1700," *Journal of the West* 5:336–354. (17, 29)

[74] Frazer, Robert. 1885. *The Apaches of the White Mountain Reservation, Arizona*. Philadelphia: Indian Rights Association. (41)

[75] Gatewood, C. B. 1929. "Lieutenant Charles B. Gatewood, 6th U.S. Cavalry and the Surrender of Geronimo." In *Proceedings of the Annual Meeting and Dinner of the Order of Indian Wars of the United States*, pp. 45-61. Washington, D.C. (41)

[76]   Gay, Dorothy Frances. 1933. "Apache
        Art." M.A. thesis, University of Arizona.   (50)

[77]   Getty, Harry T. 1963. "The San Carlos
        Indian Cattle Industry." *Anthropological
        Papers of the University of Arizona* 7.   (21, 52)

[78]   Goddard, Pliny E. 1911. "Jicarilla
        Apache Texts." *Anthropological Papers of
        the American Museum of Natural History* 8.   (45)

[79]   _____.1916. "The Masked Dancers of
        the Apache." In *Holmes Anniversary Vol-
        ume*, p. 132–136. Washington, D.C.   (49)

[80]   _____. 1919. "San Carlos Apache
        Texts." *Anthropological Papers of the
        American Museum of Natural History* 24
        (pt. 3):140–367.   (46)

[81]   _____. 1920. "White Mountain Apache
        Texts." *Anthropological Papers of the
        American Museum of Natural History* 24
        (pt. 4): 368–527.   (46)

[82]   Goodwin, Grenville. 1933. "Clans of the
        Western Apache," *New Mexico Historical
        Review* 8:176–182.   (19)

[83]   _____. 1937. "The Characteristics and
        Function of Clan in a Southern Athapas-
        can Culture," *American Anthropologist*
        39:394–407.   (20)

[84] ———. 1938. "White Mountain Apache Religion," *American Anthropologist* 40:24–37.   (47)

[85] * ———. 1942. *The Social Organization of the Western Apache*. Chicago: University of Chicago Press.   (19)

[86] ———. 1945. "A Comparison of Navaho and White Mountain Apache Ceremonial Forms and Categories," *Southwestern Journal of Anthropology* 1:498–506.   (48)

[87] ———. 1973. *Grenville Goodwin among the Western Apache: Letters from the Field*, ed. Morris E. Opler. Tucson: University of Arizona Press.   (20)

[88] Goodwin, Grenville, and Charles Kant. 1954. "A Native Religious Movement among the White Mountain and Cibecue Apache," *Southwestern Journal of Anthropology* 10:385–404.   (48)

[89] * Gunnerson, Dolores A. 1974. *The Jicarilla Apaches: A Study in Survival*. De Kalb: Northern Illinois University Press.   (24)

[90] Gunnerson, James H., and Dolores A. Gunnerson. 1971. "Apachean Culture: A Study in Unity and Diversity." In *Anthropological Papers of the University of Arizona* 21:7–27.   (19)

[91]   Hagberg, Elizabeth B. 1939. "Southwestern Indian Burial Practices." M.A.
thesis, University of Arizona.   (18)

[92]   Hall, Sharlot M. 1908. "Olive A. Oatman: Her Captivity with the Apache Indians, and Her Later Life," *Out West*
29:216–227.   (33)

[93]   Harrington, M. R. 1912. "The Devil
Dance of the Apache," *Museum Journal*
3:6–9. University of Pennsylvania.   (47, 49)

[94]   Hodge, Frederick Webb, ed. 1907–
1910. *Handbook of American Indians North
of Mexico. Bureau of American Ethnology
Bulletin* 30. 2 vols. Washington, D.C.:
Government Printing Office.   (4, 11)

[95]   Hoijer, Harry. 1938. *Chiricahua and Mescalero Apache Texts,* with ethnological
notes by Morris E. Opler. Chicago: University of Chicago Press.   (46)

[96]   _____. 1938. "The Southern Athapascan Languages," *American Anthropologist*
40:75–87.   (52)

[97]   _____. 1945-1946. "The Apachean
Verb," *International Journal of American
Linguistics* 11:193–203;   12:1–13;
51–59.   (53)

[98]   ———. 1948. "The Structure of the Noun in the Apachean Languages," *Proceedings of the International Congress of Americanists,1947* 28:173–184.   (52)

[99]   ———. ed. 1971. "The Position of the Apachean Language in the Athapaskan Stock," *Anthropological Papers of the University of Arizona* 21:3–6.   (52)

[100]   Howard, Olive O. 1907. *My Life and Experiences among Our Hostile Indians*. Hartford, Conn.: A. D. Worthington and Co. (Reprinted 1972, New York: Da Capo Press.)   (41)

[101]   Hrdlička, Aleš. 1905. "Notes on the San Carlos Apache," *American Anthropologist* 7:480–495.   (20)

[102]   Jicarilla Apache Tribe. 1937. *Constitution and By-Laws of the Jicarilla Apache Indian Reservation, New Mexico*. Approved August 4, 1937. Washington, D.C.: Government Printing Office.   (52)

[103]   ———. 1938. *Corporate Charter of the Jicarilla Apache Tribe of the Jicarilla Reservation*. Ratified September 4, 1937. Washington, D.C.: Government Printing Office.   (52)

[104]   Kane, Henry. 1937. "The Apache Secret Devil Dance," *El Palacio* 42:93–94.   (49)

[105]   Kaywaykla, James. 1961. "I Survived the Massacre of Tres Castillos," ed. Eve Ball, *True West* 8, No. 6, pp. 22, 38.   (15)

[106]   _____. 1963. "Nana's People," ed. Eve Ball. *True West* 10, No. 6, pp. 20–21, 66–67.   (15)

[107] *   _____. 1970. *In the Days of Victorio: Recollections of a Warm Springs Apache*, ed. Eve Ball. Tucson: University of Arizona Press.   (14, 28)

[108]   La Farge, Oliver. 1959. *Santa Fe: The Autobiography of a Southwestern Town*. Norman: University of Oklahoma Press.   (32)

[109]   Landar, Herbert J. 1960. "The Loss of Athapascan Words for Fish in the Southwest," *International Journal of American Linguistics* 26: 75–77.   (53)

[110]   Lockwood, Frank C. 1928. *Arizona Characters*. Los Angeles: Time-Mirror Press.   (33)

[111]   _____. 1932. *Pioneer Days in Arizona, from the Spanish Occupation to Statehood*. New York: Macmillan.   (32)

[112] * ———. 1938. *The Apache Indians*. New York: Macmillan. (17, 28)

[113] ———. 1939. "Cochise, the Noble Warrior," *Arizona Highways* 15, No. 2, 6–7, 24–27. (39)

[114] ———. 1943. *More Arizona Characters*. Tucson: University of Arizona Press.. (33)

[115] Lummis, Charles F. 1893. *The Land of Poco Tiempo*. New York: Charles Scribner's Sons. (16)

[116] ———. 1962. "Chiricahua Apache Costume in the 1880's," *The Master Key* 36:33–34. (51)

[117] McAllister, J. Gilbert. 1955. "Kiowa-Apache Social Organization." In *Social Organization of the North American Tribes*, ed. Fred Eggan, pp. 99–172. Chicago: University of Chicago Press. (26)

[118] McCord, T. T. 1946. "An Economic History of the Mescalero Apache." M.A. thesis, University of New Mexico. (23)

[119] * Mails, Thomas E. 1974. *The People Called Apache*. Englewood Cliffs, N.J.: Prentice-Hall. (17, 28)

[120] Martin, Douglas D. 1963–1966. *An Ari-*

zona Chronology. 2 vols: I. *The Territorial Years, 1846-1912;* II. *Statehood, 1913-1936.* Tucson: University of Arizona Press. (31)

[121] Matson, Daniel S., and Albert H. Schroeder, eds. 1957. "Cordero's Description of the Apache — 1796," *New Mexico Historical Review* 27: 335–356. (17, 29)

[122] Mazzanovich, Anton. 1926. *Trailing Geronimo*, ed. E. A. Brininstool. Los Angeles: Gem Publishing Co. (41)

[123] Melody, Michael E. 1976. "The Sacred Hoop: The Way of the Chiricahua Apache and Teton Lakota." Ph.D. dissertation, University of Notre Dame. (11, 22)

[124] Miles, Nelson A. 1896. *Personal Recollections and Observations of General Nelson A. Miles.* Chicago: Werner. (Reprinted 1969, New York: Da Capo Press.) (41)

[125] Moorehead, Max L. 1968. *The Apache Frontier: Jacobo Ugarte and the Spanish-Indian Relations in Northern New Spain, 1769–1791.* Norman: University of Oklahoma Press. (29)

[126] * Mulligan, R. A. 1965. "Apache Pass and Old Fort Bowie," *The Smoke Signal*, No. 11:1–24. Tucson Corral of Westerners. (37)

[127]   Myers, Lee. 1966. "The Enigma of Man-
        gas Coloradas' Death," *New Mexico His-
        torical Review* 41:287–304.   (39)

[128]   Ogle, Ralph H. 1958. "The Apache and
        the Government — 1870's," *New Mexico
        Historical Review* 33:81–102.   (39)

[129]   _____. 1970. *Federal Control of the West-
        ern Apaches, 1848–1886*. Albuquerque:
        Univeristy of New Mexico Press.   (32)

[130]   Opler, Morris E. 1935. "The Concept of
        Supernatural Power Among the
        Chiricahua and Mescalero Apaches,"
        American Anthropologist 37:65-70.   (47)

[131]   _____. 1936. "The Influence of Aborig-
        inal Pattern and White Contact on a Re-
        cently Introduced Ceremony, the Mesca-
        lero Peyote Rite," *Journal of American
        Folklore* 49:143–166.   (50)

[132]   _____. 1936. "An Interpretation of
        Ambivalence of Two American Indian
        Tribes," *Journal of Social Psychology*
        7:82–116.   (27)

[133]   _____. 1936. "The Kinship Systems of
        the Southern Athabaskan-Speaking
        Tribes," *American Anthropologist*
        38:620–633.   (27)

[134]   _____. 1936. "Rule and Practice in the

Behavior Between Jicarilla Affinal Relatives," *American Anthropologist* 38:453–454. (24)

[135]   _____. 1936. "A Summary of Jicarilla Apache Culture," *American Anthropologist* 38:202–223. (24)

[136]   _____. 1938. *Myths and Tales of the Jicarilla Apache Indians. Memoirs of the American Folklore Society* 31. (45)

[137]*   _____. 1938. "The Sacred Clowns of the Chiricahua and Mescalero Indians," *El Palacio* 44:75–79. (47)

[138]   _____. 1938. "The Use of Peyote by the Carrizo and Lipan Apache Tribes," *American Anthropologist* 40:271–285. (48)

[139]   _____. 1940. *Myths and Legends of the Lipan Apache Indians. Memoirs of the American Folklore Society* 36. (45)

[140]   _____. 1940. "The Raid and War-Path Language of the Chiricahua Apache," *American Anthropologist* 42:617–634. (50)

[141]*   _____. 1941. *An Apache Life-Way; The Economic, Social, and Religious Institutions of the Chiricahua Indians*. Chicago: University of Chicago Press. (22, 46)

[142]   ———. 1942. "Adolescence Rite of the Jicarilla," *El Palacio* 49:25–38.   (49)

[143]   ———. 1942. *Myths and Tales of the Chiricahua Apache Indians. Memoirs of the American Folklore Society* 37.   (45)

[144]   ———. 1943. "The Character and Derivation of the Jicarilla Holiness Rite," *University of New Mexico Bulletin, Anthropological Series* 4, No. 3.   (50)

[145]   ———. 1943. "Navaho Shamanistic Practice among the Jicarilla Apache," *New Mexico Anthropologist* 6-7:13–18.   (24, 50)

[146]   ———. 1945. "The Lipan Apache Death Complex and Its Extensions," *Southwestern Journal of Anthropology* 1:122–141.   (48)

[147]   ———. 1945. "Themes as Dynamic Forces in Culture," *American Journal of Sociology* 51:198–206.   (27)

[148]   ———. 1946. *Childhood and Youth in Jicarilla Apache Society. Publications of the Frederick Webb Hodge Anniversary Publication Fund* 5. Los Angeles: The Southwest Museum.   (50)

[149]   ———. 1946. "Chiricahua Apache

Material Relating to Sorcery," *Primitive Man* 19:81–92.   (47)

[150]   _____. 1946. "The Creative Role of Shamanism in Mescalero Apache Mythology," *Journal of American Folklore* 59:268–281.   (47)

[151]   _____. 1946. "Mountain Spirits of the Chiricahua," *The Masterkey* 20:125–131.   (47)

[152]   _____. 1946. "Reaction to Death among the Mescalero Apache," *Southwestern Journal of Anthropology* 2:454–467.   (48)

[153]   _____. 1947. "Notes on Chiricahua Apache Culture. 1. Supernatural Power and the Shaman," *Primitive Man* 20:1–14.   (22, 47)

[154]*   _____. 1955. "An Outline of Chiricahua Apache Social Organization." In *Social Organization of North American Tribes*, ed. Fred Eggan, pp. 173-239. Chicago: University of Chicago Press.   (22)

[155]   _____. 1960. "Myth and Practice in Jicarilla Apache Eschatology," *Journal of American Folklore* 73:133–153.   (48)

[156]   _____. 1968. "Remuneration to Supernaturals and Man in Apachean Ceremonialism," *Ethnology* 7:356–393.   (47)

[157]* ———. 1969. *Apache Odyssey: A Journey between Two Worlds*. New York: Holt, Rinehart and Winston.   (15)

[158] ———.1971. "Jicarilla Apache Territory, Economy, and Society in 1850," *Southwestern Journal of Anthropology* 27:309–329.   (24)

[159] ———. 1971. "Pots, Apache, and the Dismal River Culture Aspect," *Anthropological Papers of the University of Arizona* 21:29–33.   (24)

[160] Opler, Morris E., and William E. Bittle. 1961. "The Death Practices and Eschatology of the Kiowa Apache," *Southwestern Journal of Anthropology* 17:383–394.   (48)

[161] Opler, Morris E., and Catherine H. Opler. 1950. "Mescalero Apache History in the Southwest," *New Mexico Historical Review* 25:1–36.   (23)

[162] Palmer, Edward. 1878. "Notes on Indian Manners and Customs," *American Naturalist* 12:308–313.   (17)

[163] Parmee, Edward A. 1968. *Formal Education and Culture Change: A Modern Apache Indian Community and Government*

Education Programs. Tucson: University of Arizona Press.   (21)

[164]   Pattie, James O. 1905. "Pattie's Personal Narrative of a Voyage to the Pacific and in Mexico: June 20, 1824 - August 30, 1830." In *Early Western Travels*, ed. Reuben Gold Thwaites, 18:23–324. Cleveland: Arthur H. Clark Co.   (17)

[165]   Pollard, William G. 1965. "Structure and Stress: Social Change among the Fort Sill Apache and Their Ancestors, 1870–1960." M.A. thesis, University of Oklahoma.   (22)

[166]   Reagan, Albert B. 1903. "Naëzhosh; or, the Apache Pole Game," *Proceedings of the Indiana Academy of Science* (1902):68–71.   (21)

[167]   _____. 1904. "The Apache Stick Game," *Proceedings of the Indiana Academy of Science* (1903):197–199.   (20)

[168]   _____. 1905. "The Apache Medicine Game," *Proceedings of the Indiana Academy of Science* (1904):285–286.   (21)

[169]   _____. 1905. "The Moccasin Game," *Proceedings of the Indiana Academy of Science* (1904):289–292.   (20)

[170]   _____. 1930. "Notes on the Indians of

the Fort Apache Region," *Anthropological Papers of the American Museum of Natural History* 31 (pt. 5):281–345. (20)

[171] Roberts, Helen H. 1929. "Basketry of the San Carlos Apache," *Anthropological Papers of the American Museum of Natural History* 31 (pt.2):121–218. (51)

[172] Roe, Frank G. 1955. *The Indian and the Horse*. Norman: University of Oklahoma Press. (30)

[173] Sacks, Benjamin H., ed. 1962. "New Evidence on the Bascom Affair," *Arizona and the West* 4:261–278. (36)

[174] San Carlos Apache Tribe. 1936. *Constitution and By-Laws of the San Carlos Apache Tribe, Arizona*. Approved January 17, 1936. Washington, D.C.: Government Printing Office. (52)

[175] ———. 1941. *Corporate Charter of the San Carlos Apache Tribe, Arizona*, ratified October 16, 1940. Washington, D.C.: Government Printing Office. (52)

[176] Schellie, Don. 1968. *Vast Domain of Blood: The Story of the Camp Grant Massacre*. Los Angeles: Westernlore Press. (39)

[177] Schliesser, Paul. 1952. "The Apache

Mutiny of 1881 Echoes in the Death of Napas the Scout," *The Apache Lutheran (Apache Scout)* 30:70–72. (39)

[178]* Schwatka, Frederick. 1887. "Among the Apaches," *Century Magazine* 34 (May):41–52. (16)

[179] Secoy, Frank. 1953. *Changing Military Patterns on the Great Plains (17th Century Through Early 19th Century). American Ethnological Society Monograph* 21. (30)

[180] Sjoberg, Andrée F. 1953. "Lipan Apache Culture in Historical Perspective," *Southwestern Journal of Anthropology* 9:76–98. (26)

[181] Smart, Charles. 1868. "Notes on the 'Tonto' Apaches," *Annual Report of the Smithsonian Institution* (1867), pp. 417–419. Washington, D.C.: Government Printing Office. (20)

[182] Smith, Cornelius C. Jr. 1967. *William Sanders Oury; History-Maker of the Southwest*. Tucson: University of Arizona Press. (32)

[183] Smith, Ralph A. "The Scalp Hunt in Chihuahua — 1849," *New Mexico Historical Review* 40:117–140. (31)

[184]   [Smithsonian Institution]. 1974. *North American Indians: Photographs from the National Anthropological Archives*. Chicago: University of Chicago Press.

[185]*   Sonnichsen, Charles Leland. 1973. *The Mescalero Apaches*. 2d ed. Norman: University of Oklahoma Press.   (25, 52)

[186]   Spicer, Edward H. 1962. *Cycles of Conquest: The Impact of Spain, Mexico, and the United States on the Indians of the Southwest, 1533–1960*. Tucson: University of Arizona Press.   (17)

[187]   Spring, John A. 1966. *John Spring's Arizona*, ed. A. M. Gustafson. Tucson: University of Arizona Press.   (32)

[188]   Swanton, John R. 1952. *The Indian Tribes of North America. Bureau of American Ethnology Bulletin* 145. Washington, D.C.: Government Printing Office.   (11)

[189]*   Tanner, Clara Lee. 1947. "Spirits Which Come Out of the Mountains," *Arizona Highways* 23, No.7:38–39.   (49)

[190]   Taylor, Fenton. 1960. "The West's Bloodiest Pass," *True West* 7, No.4:6-10, 38-41.   (38)

[191]*   Terrell, John Upton. 1972. *Apache*

Chronicle. New York: World Publishing
Co.   (28, 31)

[192]   Tevis, James H. 1954. *Arizona in the '50's*.
Albuquerque: University of New Mexico
Press.   (37)

[193]*   Thrapp, Dan. L. 1964. *Al Sieber, Chief of
Scouts*. Norman: University of Oklahoma
Press.   (34)

[194]*   _____. 1967. *The Conquest of Apacheria*.
Norman: University of Oklahoma Press.   (34)

[195]   _____. 1972. *General Crook and the Sierra
Madre Adventure*. Norman: University of
Oklahoma Press.   (35)

[196]   _____. 1973. "Juh: An Incredible Indian," *Southwestern Studies* 39:1–44.   (35)

[197]*   _____. 1974. *Victorio and the Mimbres
Apaches*. Norman: University of Oklahoma Press.   (34)

[198]   _____. 1976. "A Man Called
Geronimo," *Arizona Highways* 52, No.
5:2-11.   (35)

[199]   Tiller, Veronica. 1976. "The History of
the Jicarilla Apache Tribe, 1541–1970."
Ph.D. dissertation, University of New
Mexico.   (24)

[200]   Tyler, Barbara Ann. 1965. "Cochise: Apache War Leader, 1858–1861," *Journal of Arizona History* 6:1-10. United States. Indian Claims Commission. 1974. *American Indian Ethnohistory: Indians of the Southwest*; comp. and ed. David Agee Horr. New York: Garland Publishing Co.
(38)

[201]   ———. Homer Aschmann, "Environment and Ecology in the 'Northern Tonto' Claim Area." *Apache Indians V*.
(21)

[202]   ———. Elizabeth V. Atwater, "The Jicarilla Apaches, 1601–1849." *Apache Indians VIII*.
(25)

[203]   ———. Harry W. Basehart, "Mescalero Apache Subsistence Patterns and Socio-Political Organization." *Apache Indians XII*.
(23, 52)

[204]   ———. Averam Bender, "A Study of the Jicarilla Apache Indians, 1846–1887." *Apache Indians IX*.
(36)

[205]   ———. Averam Bender, "A Study of the Mescalero Apache Indians, 1846–1880." *Apache Indians XI*.
(23)

[206]   ———. Averam Bender, "A Study of Western Apache Indians, 1846–1886." *Apache Indians V*.
(35)

[207]   _____. Donald Cutter, "Indian Land Rights in the Jicarilla Apache Area." *Apache Indians VI*.   (35)

[208]   _____. Burton Le Roy Gordon, "Environment, Settlement, and Land Use in the Jicarilla Apache Claim Area." *Apache Indians VI*.   (25)

[209]   _____. Kenneth F. Neighbours, "Government, Land, and Indian Policies Relative to Lipan, Mescalero, and Tigua Indians." *Apache Indians III*.   (35)

[210]   _____. Jean W. Nelson, "Anthropological Material on the Jicarilla Apaches." *Apache Indians VIII*.   (25)

[211]   _____. Morris E. Opler, "Lipan and Mescalero Apache in Texas." *Apache Indians X*.   (23, 26)

[212]   _____. Verne F. Ray, "Ethnohistorical Analysis of Documents Relating to the Apache Indians of Texas." *Apache Indians X*.   (30)

[213]   _____. Albert Schroeder, "A Study of the Apache Indian." *Apache Indians I, IV*.   (22)

[214]   _____. Alfred B. Thomas, "The Jicarilla Apache Indians: A History, 1598–1888." *Apache Indians VIII*.   (25, 30)

[215]   ———. Alfred B. Thomas, "The Mescal-
         ero Apache, 1653–1874." *Apache Indians*
         XI.   (23, 30)

[216]   Utley, Robert M. 1961. "The Bascom Af-
         fair: A Reconstruction," *Arizona and the*
         West 3:59–68.   (36)

[217]   Vanderwerth, W. C., comp. 1971. *Indian*
         Oratory: Famous Speeches by Noted Indian
         Chieftains. Norman: University of Okla-
         homa Press.   (13)

[218]   White Mountain Apache Tribe of the
         Fort Apache Indian Reservation, Ari-
         zona. 1938. *Constitution and By-Laws. . . .*
         Approved   August   26,   1938.
         Washington, D.C.: Government Print-
         ing Office.   (52)

[219]   Wilson, H. Clyde. 1964. "Jicarilla
         Apache Political and Economic Struc-
         tures" *University of California Publications*
         in American Archaeology and Ethnology
         48(4):297–360.   (24)

[220]   Woody, Clara T. 1962. "The Woolsey
         Expeditions of 1864," *Arizona and the*
         West 4:157–176.   (39)

[221]   Worcester, Donald E. 1941. "The Be-
         ginnings of the Apache Menace of the

Southwest," *New Mexico Historical Review* 16:1–14.   (31)

[222]   _____. 1941. "Early Spanish Accounts of the Apache Indians," *American Anthropologist* 43:308–312.   (29)

[223]   _____. 1944–1945. "The Spread of Spanish Horses in the Southwest, 1700–1800," *New Mexico Historical Review* 19:225–232; 20:1–13.   (30)